Living Independently

on the

Autism Spectrum

What you need to know to move into a place of your own, succeed at work, start a relationship, stay safe, and *Enjoy Life as an Adult on the Autism Spectrum*

LYNNE SORAYA

Author of *Psychology Today's Asperger's Diary*

Avon, Massachusetts

Copyright © 2013 by F+W Media, Inc.
All rights reserved.
This book, or parts thereof, may not be reproduced in any form without permission from the publisher; exceptions are made for brief excerpts used in published reviews.

Published by
Adams Media, a division of F+W Media, Inc.
57 Littlefield Street, Avon, MA 02322. U.S.A.
www.adamsmedia.com

ISBN 10: 1-4405-5764-0
ISBN 13: 978-1-4405-5764-4
eISBN 10: 1-4405-5765-9
eISBN 13: 978-1-4405-5765-1

Printed in the United States of America.

10   9   8   7   6   5   4   3   2   1

This book is intended as general information only, and should not be used to diagnose or treat any health condition. In light of the complex, individual, and specific nature of health problems, this book is not intended to replace professional medical advice. The ideas, procedures, and suggestions in this book are intended to supplement, not replace, the advice of a trained medical professional. Consult your physician before adopting any of the suggestions in this book, as well as about any condition that may require diagnosis or medical attention. The author and publisher disclaim any liability arising directly or indirectly from the use of this book.

Many of the designations used by manufacturers and sellers to distinguish their product are claimed as trademarks. Where those designations appear in this book and F+W Media was aware of a trademark claim, the designations have been printed with initial capital letters.

This book is available at quantity discounts for bulk purchases.
For information, please call 1-800-289-0963.

Contents

Praise for Living Independently on the Autism Spectrum

"Being able to live a happy, safe, creative, and self-supporting life is the fondest hope for people on the spectrum. Lynne Soraya's book is a must-read for autistic people and those who love them." ~Steve Silberman, editor of *Wired* magazine and author of *NeuroTribes*

"A practical, empathic guide for adults with ASD. This book is a must-read for adults with ASD, their families, and those committed to educate, support, and mentor them." ~Sam Goldstein, PhD, author of *Raising Resilient Children with Autism Spectrum Disorders*

"Lynne Soraya provides a comprehensive blueprint for building a life, from managing finances and housekeeping to navigating the complex social dynamics of love and friendship." ~Carlin Flora, author of *Friendfluence*

"Lynne distills important advice into a readable and practical text that is anchored both by her own experience and by the voices of other autistic individuals." ~Landon Bryce, founder of ThAutcast.com and author of *I Love Being My Own Autistic Self*

"Straightforward, inspiring, and packed with useful tips that will help adults who are on the autism spectrum to gain confidence and enjoy their lives." ~Alice Boyes, PhD, *Psychology Today* blogger

"I would highly recommend this book to not only autistic adults but also to parents, teachers, therapists, and human resource managers, as it provides the kind of insight into autism that only an autistic person can provide." ~Kym Grosso, MBA, *Psychology Today* blogger and founder of AutismInRealLife.com

"Lynne Soraya has put together a lovely guidebook for supporting autistic people in their journey toward self-awareness, independence, and day-to-day success." ~Shannon Des Roches Rosa, editor of *Thinking Person's Guide to Autism*

Introduction

Going out on your own can be an exciting challenge for anyone. It can be scary, but it can also be wonderful.

For those of us on the autism spectrum, it can be even more daunting. We can face difficulties that others don't even think about. The stress of change and transition can be particularly acute. But, like anyone else, we have our strengths. It's just a question of finding and harnessing them.

Like many who grew up undiagnosed, I struggled through those times alone, without an understanding of why I encountered so many issues. I made plenty of mistakes. If you're reading this book, you've got something going for you: You're arming yourself with knowledge. That is a great start.

In this book, you'll expand your knowledge and draw on the collective experiences of people on the spectrum who've found their way through this transition. This book will help you to learn what you need to know in order to survive and thrive on the autism spectrum.

Read on for some of the important topics we will cover.

We will talk about soft skills, like understanding yourself. What are your skills and abilities? How can you best tap them? Then we will move on to understanding others. Why do people do what they do? What are the differences in communication that can lead to challenges in connecting? What are the best ways to address these challenges?

Once you have identified some of your strengths and challenges, we will also look at building some key strategies for growth. In what areas do you want to improve your skills? What skills are required to achieve what you want in life? Out in the world, there's a lot of pressure to conform. You'll need to know how to manage your differences, and balance those pressures with your personal needs.

The world can be overwhelming to many of us. Inevitably, you will run into some stress. What are some ways to deal with those stresses? This stress may be increased by the differences in how people on the autism spectrum experience the world. We will discuss how to translate your experience of the world to others, to clearly communicate your wants and needs.

Many aspects of living on the spectrum can make us extra vulnerable to danger. We'll talk about what some of those things are, and how to best keep yourself safe. This will include choosing where to live, the right kind of living situation, and building a support system. In a home and work environment, some routine skills may be more difficult for us, such as time management, organization, and getting around. We'll talk about each of these areas, and talk about how to overcome some of these challenge areas.

The employment world can be a particularly difficult one for those on the spectrum. We'll discuss the many different aspects of finding the kind of work that will work for you. We'll talk about setting career goals, identifying job opportunities, handling the unique challenges of the job interview, and the complex challenges of handling the social aspects of the workplace.

Going out on your own brings new challenges in terms of developing new relationships, and managing changes in existing ones. We'll talk about how your family relationships may change, and how they *should* change. We'll discuss when you should ask for support, and when it will be necessary to set boundaries.

Making friends is a common challenge experienced by many on the spectrum. Once the structure of school is over, making friends can be even more difficult. We'll cover changes in your social circle, ways to make friends, and how to keep them. Most of all, we'll talk about dating and romantic relationships. What are the ins and outs of dating? And what about that all important word—sex?

A Few of the People You Will Meet

Some of the best teachers I've met in life are the diverse members of the autism community: other adults on the autism spectrum, families of those on the spectrum, and experts who have made autism their life's work. In this book, you'll meet a number of these people. They will share with you their insights on how a person on the spectrum can learn to tackle the challenges of his condition and how to live a successful, happy life on the spectrum.

To start us off, I asked them a question: If you had the opportunity to speak to a person on the spectrum who's just starting out in life, what *one* thing would you want to say to this person?

Here are some of their responses:

- "Success has little to do with your circumstances and everything to do with your strategies." Brian R. King, Adult on the Autism Spectrum, parent, licensed clinical social worker, author of *Strategies for Building Successful Relationships with People on the Autism Spectrum*

- "Take lots of long walks by yourself. What [a diagnosis] *means* to you is something only you will know, so you need the guts to face things honestly. And never process all this at anyone else's speed (or wishes) other than your own." Michael John Carley, Adult on the Autism Spectrum, parent, executive director of the Global and Regional Asperger Syndrome Partnership, and author of *Asperger's from the Inside Out*

- "It's a label, not a limitation—you can be anything you want to be because you'll always be an individual." Gavin Bollard, Adult on the Autism Spectrum, parent, and blogger at *Life with Aspergers (http://life-with-aspergers.blogspot.com)*

- "Learn how to make yourself happy. You will have far more successes and far more satisfaction and happiness if you put in the work on your relationship with your self first." Amy K. Alward, PhD, Adult on the Autism Spectrum

- "Gaining your independence brings a whole new set of challenges, but the majority are surmountable. The first thing you need is a good sense of self-awareness. With good self-awareness, you can surmount some issues, find workarounds for others, and explain your ways in a manner that other people can understand." Ennien Ashbrook, Adult on the Autism Spectrum, investment finance assistant, performance dancer, and blogger at *Snakedancing (http://snakedance.tumblr.com)*

This is a time that can be difficult, but it's also a time of challenge, opportunity, and growth. Welcome to an exciting phase of your life!

About This Text

Idioms/Expressions
In the text of the book, I, and some of the other contributors, have used idioms. For your reference, I've included a list of these idioms and their meanings as an appendix at the end of this book.

Pronouns
In several instances I have simply used "he" or "she," rather than the clumsy phrase "he or she." This is for the sake for brevity and flow of the text. When reading these sections, please keep in mind that the advice presented is intended to be valid for either gender.

CHAPTER 1

Skills for Self-Advocacy

When you talk to adults on the autism spectrum, one of the biggest challenges many of them will tell you they've faced is figuring out other human beings. For us, other people's behavior can be very confusing. A crucial skill is to become familiar with the way others think, how it may vary from how you think, and how to navigate through those differences and advocate for your own needs.

In this chapter, we will go through some of the ways you can do this, beginning with understanding yourself. In order to effectively self-advocate, you will need to be able to know what you need, as well as what skills and abilities you already possess. This will tell you what tools you have to work with.

Likewise, it's important to understand what people expect from you, and how those expectations fit with your skills and abilities. Where there are gaps, you will need to bridge them. It will also be important to understand your own limits and preferences, and when to say no.

Those of us on the spectrum face strong pressures to be able to do everything in the same way everyone else does. It's important to recognize when that is destructive to your own well-being. You'll want to continue to build competencies, while still being kind to yourself. We will talk about some of the considerations to make in order to decide when enough is enough.

Self-Advocacy Through Self-Knowledge

Rachel Cohen-Rottenberg is a wife and mom, a writer, and a disability rights activist who has written three books: *A Sense of Place: The Story of the Williams Family Farm*, *The Uncharted Path: My Journey with Late-Diagnosed Autism*, *Blazing My Trail: Living and Thriving with Autism*. She also compiled and edited *We've Been Here All Along: Autistics Over 35 Speak Out in Poetry and Prose*. Recently, I interviewed Rachel regarding her experiences with understanding other people's behavior as an adult with autism.

Here's what she had to say:

"I've always had that feeling that there is a 'hidden conversation' going on, and since my diagnosis, I've realized why I feel that way: the 'hidden conversation' is happening nonverbally, and I can't parse nonverbals in real time. I can think of a number of times when I was first on my own that I got into potential trouble, mainly with people I was interested in romantically who could have hurt me if they hadn't been decent people.

At a certain point, I was fortunate to have friends who saw that I was rather innocent, and who would let me know who was trustworthy and who wasn't. I relied on friends like that in the early years of being on my own. After awhile, I began to realize that I'm a very astute observer when I can get some distance and look at the process of what is going on. I learned that instead of assuming that people were straightforward like me, I had to stop and watch them before I got involved with them. I began to realize that when I am outside of an interaction, I can see very clearly how the interaction works, so I began to use that to my advantage and get a good long look at people before I got close to them. I also learned that no matter what the interaction, I had to stop and get some space and think before committing to a decision, because I was very prone to getting swept along in other people's emotions. I became very cautious and very observant, and I learned very good personal boundaries. They have all served me well."

Building Self-Awareness

When you get out into the workplace, and other adult environments, one of the most important things you will need to learn to do is to self-advocate. In order to do this, you will need to be able to identify your needs and be able to clearly articulate them. This is why getting to know yourself is so important.

Attaining self-knowledge can be difficult for some people on the spectrum, for a number of reasons. Some of these may have to do with aspects of autism itself, or they may have to do with the pressures of others, or a little of both.

Internal Pressures

Those of us on the autism spectrum face some additional challenges when it comes to self-knowledge.

Those not on the autism spectrum are far more likely to see models of self-awareness being modeled in ways that work for them. Many of these skills are transferable, and thus can be learned from someone who does not have autism. However, there may be slight differences in what works optimally for someone who isn't on the spectrum versus someone who is.

Second, and maybe more crucially, is that many of us on the spectrum may have neurological issues, such as alexithymia or sensory issues, which make self-awareness difficult. Alexithymia is a condition affecting many on the autism spectrum that makes it difficult to recognize and respond to your own emotional states. This can create difficulties in identifying your own needs. If you can't identify the feeling of being upset, how do you identify the root causes of that upset? If you cannot identify the root causes, how do you advocate in such a way so as to prevent such stress in the future?

Sensory issues impact most of us on the spectrum in many different ways. Combinations of different types of sensory input may be overwhelming, which can make it further difficult to identify emotions or physical discomfort. For some (like me), emotions and sensory experiences can be interrelated; a feeling of being overwhelmed in just one of these two areas can lead to overload in the other.

IN OUR OWN WORDS

I need to consciously monitor my emotional state, in a similar way as someone with numbness [who] needs to watch for [the] danger [of unintentionally injuring themselves]. It's not that I'm not feeling these emotions or that they're not affecting me, but I'm not aware of what's going on until things boil over one way or another. —David Cameron Staples, Adult on the Autism Spectrum

External Pressures

Everyone feels external pressures to conform to what other people want. Those who have grown up feeling isolated and alone may feel these pressures even more so. It's common to want to be liked. But, it should not be for something that you are not.

It's important to recognize when you find yourself being pressured into being differently than how you typically are in a way that is destructive. Only you can truly decide who you want to be. No one can dictate this to you, though some may try. Don't let them.

A lot of self-awareness will come with life experience, but there are some ways that you can help it along. What works for you may vary—as we are all unique. Read on for ideas.

Cultivating Mindfulness

There are a number of techniques that are designed to enhance *mindfulness*. Mindfulness is often described in a simplistic way as "living in the moment." Learning to be mindful is learning to focus your attention on your feelings, body, physical surroundings, and experience at this exact moment in time.

When you do this effectively you will also learn to screen out information that distracts from that attention. This is a skill set that's extremely helpful for those of us who often find the "noise" of this world (and our strong sensory reaction to it) overwhelming. Learning to screen out this "noise" makes it much easier to become aware of our own internal feelings and reactions, and therefore, makes it easier for us to make the appropriate adjustments to them.

Disciplines like meditation, yoga, or the martial arts can help to build mindfulness, but sometimes discovery is as simple as asking a question. You can start with "what" questions:

- What do you like?

- What do you not like?

- What do you do well?

- What is more of a struggle for you?

Once you have answered these questions, you can follow them up with "why" questions:

- Why do you like what you like?

- Why do you dislike what you dislike?

- Why are you good at what you are good at?

- Why are certain things more of a struggle?

The answers to these questions can provide clues to the strategies you may want to use to address challenges. For example, say you struggle with cooking. Why is that? Is it because you have trouble with fine motor skills and fear cutting or burning yourself? Do you have trouble with the multitasking and organizational skills involved? Or is it just that you have trouble reading cookbooks, because you don't know the terminology?

Each of these issues may need a separate solution. If you worry about burning or cutting yourself, what are some solutions?

- You can buy premade foods that can be heated up in a microwave, versus over an open flame

- You can buy precut meats and vegetables so that you will not need to handle knives

- You can eat out, or buy premade salads

- If you share cooking responsibilities, you can negotiate with the other person to split the tasks according to your strengths: Perhaps you assemble the salads and marinate the chicken, while she cuts the vegetables.

In Our Own Words

The more you understand your own neurology, the better off you are. —Judy Endow, MSW, Adult on the Autism Spectrum, speaker, and author of several books, including *Learning the Hidden Curriculum: The Odyssey of One Autistic Adult*

Learning about Your Personality

A more structured way of asking yourself questions is to take tests designed to identify your personality type, along with your strengths and interests. A typical test like this, used by many organizations, is the Myers-Briggs test.

The first thing this type of test tells you about is how you relate to people. Are you an extrovert (someone who is outgoing) or an introvert (someone who is more reserved)? Many make the assumption that those on the spectrum cannot be an extrovert, but many people on the spectrum (and their families) would argue otherwise. A person can have a strong desire to be with others, but yet struggle with making it happen. Those who have this strong desire to connect may have a higher level of stress, because of the difference between how much they want to socialize and how successfully they are able to achieve it.

Another thing that this type of test can teach you is how you go about solving problems and processing information. Once you go out into the world, understanding this (and the different ways people can go about it) can be crucial—especially in the workplace. It can impact what types of people you interact best with, and can help you in choosing how to communicate about yourself to someone who is different than you.

Seeking the Input of Others

There are times when others can see what we don't, especially when we are under stress. In such situations, it may be appropriate to ask someone you consider trustworthy for feedback. A number of adults have reported to me that their friends and loved ones can often sense signs of trouble before they do (particularly among those who have issues with alexithymia).

Those who live closely with you may be able to identify patterns in your behavior you weren't previously aware of. This can be helpful in identifying "hidden" sources of stress, or simply patterns in behavior that are potentially problematic in specific situations. Many people (neurotypical people included) have "tells"—specific body language or facial expressions that we may not be aware of, but which serve as indicators of stress.

If you find that you still don't have the level of understanding about yourself that you'd like, you may find it valuable to seek out help from professionals such as counselors, psychologists, and psychiatrists. Part of the training individuals in these professions receive is to guide others in the types of self-awareness techniques we've discussed in this section. In addition, they may be able to guide you with suggestions for steps to use in specific situations, developing coping mechanisms, and by suggesting new ways to navigate situations you find challenging.

There are a number of factors in choosing a professional to work with. Professionals have specific areas of expertise, and focuses. It's important to choose a professional whose style and approach meshes well with your needs. Factors to consider may include things such as education, type of professional, focus of practice, and experience with those on the spectrum.

Psychiatrists, who are medical doctors, may be more focused on medication, or medical considerations, whereas a psychologist or counselor may look at behavioral causes and treatments when looking at anxiety, depression, or other challenges. If you are looking for help with problems of everyday living, or for techniques to change how you approach problems, a psychologist or counselor my suit you just fine. However, you may want to seek a psychiatrist when you need someone who is a specialist in a particular area or for help with issues that have a physical cause or that may require close monitoring of medication.

Also, consider the professional's particular area of specialty and her approach. Does she focus primarily on counseling families and couples, or on counseling individuals? Or does she do both? Is the professional experienced in working with those on the spectrum? How does she approach issues like anxiety or depression? Does she talk about feelings, or does she use techniques to help you identify and change troublesome thought patterns and approaches? What you are most comfortable with may determine which professional you choose.

Understanding Expectations

The other side of self-advocacy is learning about other people and their expectations of you. This can be particularly challenging for many of us on the spectrum, as there are a number of aspects of common social situations that are assumed but not stated. For those of us who have a hard time "reading between the lines" to identify the unspoken expectations of others, this can be very difficult.

Trouble with the "unwritten rules" is probably not new to you. Most of us have experienced it all through our lives. However, the penalties for not understanding such rules become more severe as we get older. When you are a child, if you misunderstand a teacher's expectations, you may get detention or you may get reprimanded. In the adult world, misunderstanding the expectations of an authority figure could mean losing your job, or even getting arrested.

Some Ways to Learn about Other People

Interacting with neurotypical people (those not on the autism spectrum) can be very much like interacting with someone who does not share your language and culture—what they say and do may have very different meanings from what you might expect, and vice versa. What can make such interactions particularly difficult is that many people are not *aware* of the differences, especially if they are not aware of or familiar with your diagnosis. Because of this, they will apply their own expectations to your behavior, which can lead to misunderstandings and negative outcomes.

One way to deal with this dynamic is to do what you can to understand the types of expectations most people have about social behavior. Becoming aware of their perspectives will allow you to know when you need to communicate differences, or when to adjust your behavior to avoid misinterpretation. It may also help to make people seem less confusing.

Observation

Temple Grandin, a famous professor and adult on the autism spectrum, has often said that living as a person with autism is like being an "anthropologist on mars." I know I have often felt the same. Her comparison is particularly interesting, because one of the ways that I've learned to read other people has been through "people watching"—watching social interactions as if I were an anthropologist studying an alien culture.

Many people on the spectrum have a particular ability with patterns. This is one autistic strength that can be helpful in learning how to get on in the world. If you apply yourself to paying attention to how other people interact with each other, you may be able to identify certain patterns and trends that you can utilize in relating to others.

This can be particularly helpful when you find yourself in a new environment—say, entering a new workplace or social group. Do they use certain types of language and phrases? How do they greet one another—with a handshake or a pat on the back? In online interactions, how do they use specific greetings or salutations? Observing these patterns can be particularly helpful in learning how to "fit in"—or how to be best understood.

Why is this important? I liken it to interacting with someone who doesn't share your language and culture. If you need to communicate, and they don't "speak" your language (in terms of understanding your speech and behavior patterns or body language), then you want to try to build a basic competency in their language so that you can be understood. Having that capacity gives you more options. Hopefully over time you will be able to help them to become familiar with your "language," but until then, you will at least have the ability to communicate.

You will, however, need to be careful about how you watch people. As an adult, people may be made uncomfortable if you single them out for unexpected attention. You can do some routine people watching just by noticing patterns while you interact with someone, which will appear more natural. If you decide to people watch just to people watch, you will need to be very careful how you go about it.

What Not to Do

- Do not stare. Staring is often perceived as hostile, threatening, or predatory in nature. Looking at any one person for more than a few seconds may make people feel you are "creepy" or "dangerous." Keep plenty of distance from the individual or group you're observing (if you are not interacting with them directly), and do not observe for an extended period of time. These rules apply to observing individuals or small groups.

- Do not watch people inside a building or enclosed space through a window or fence or use technology to remotely do so—people like their privacy. If you observe people in an enclosed space where they expect privacy, such as their home, you will be violating their boundaries. This will at the very least offend people and make them very uncomfortable, and at worst, it may get you arrested. It's best not to do it.

- Do not ask strangers why they do certain things. Though you may be curious, if you don't know the person, approaching him to ask why he behaved this way will make him uncomfortable.

- It may be appropriate to take a neurotypical friend or family member with you to guide you, ask questions of, and tell you when your behavior is inappropriate. It will be important, though, that he understands what you are doing and why. Let him know that you want to casually "people watch" to learn how people act, and that you want him to come along to help you.

- Keep your segments of people watching very short—you may want to bring an activity that's appropriate to the environment and stop periodically to do that activity. For example, if you're at a mall, you may stop at a bench and people watch for ten minutes, then go back to shopping, or you may read a book or work on your laptop. This will minimize the chances that you are perceived as "dangerous." If you are the type of person who is easily engrossed, you may want to set a reminder on your cell phone or other device and make sure that you honor the time limit you set for yourself.

- Choose your environment carefully—public places with a lot of people are good places to people watch, provided you minimize behavior that may make people believe you're a threat. Remember that in some environments, like a shopping mall, there may be law enforcement professionals or security guards around who are watching for criminals. Watching a person or place for too long, or staying in one place for a long time, may be seen by them as warning signs of criminal behavior. This is because criminals may linger in a specific area to watch a person or place to assess vulnerabilities and plan their attack. You don't want people to believe that this is what you are doing.

- If you are asked to leave, do so politely and quietly. If they are asking you to leave, this means they may think you are dangerous. If you get angry or argue with them, they may call the police and have you arrested. If the person asking you to leave is an authority figure, such as a policeman, this is doubly important, because resisting may result in not only arrest but in the police using violence to subdue you. You may or may not agree with their asking you to leave, but what is most important is ensuring your safety. Keep yourself calm, be respectful and polite (using terms like "Yes, sir" or "Yes, ma'am"), and leave to go on to something else, somewhere else.

Theater

Many adults on the spectrum have found taking acting or theater classes to be helpful for a number of reasons. One of the most important is that theater classes are an environment where the type of "people watching" discussed previously is directly taught. Because the aim of acting is to be able to convincingly play another person—and to convey that person's thoughts and feelings to an audience using voice, body language, and words—it is one of the few places where body language and unwritten rules will likely be talked about explicitly. They are part of the curriculum.

In Our Own Words

I, for one, have found theatre very helpful . . . immersion in drama (and literature more broadly) has probably made it easier for me to figure other people out. Drama and literature provided me with templates of human reactions to various situations on which I could draw when trying to read people in circumstances analogous to those in a given play or novel. —Jack, Adult on the Autism Spectrum and history professor

In addition, some acting techniques, such as "method acting," place emphasis on knowing and replicating in yourself the emotions of the character you're performing. These classes will often involve reading screenplays, or viewing scenes, then talking about what the character in that scene is thinking or feeling, and how that would be expressed through body language and voice tone. Often, you will not only go through this process yourself, but you will hear others talking about it, and see them acting it out. You will also get feedback as to what your body language conveys to others.

This gives you a window into the range of what other people think and feel in specific situations, and how that may differ from how you would react. What you find is that there is a great deal of variability in how individuals think and respond to a specific set of circumstances (or how they think others would respond). This can be very comforting to learn in a world that often presents only one "right" way to be. We are *all* unique, those with a neurotypical makeup and those with autism alike.

Theater can have some other particular benefits for those of us on the spectrum:

- Inclusion in a creative and welcoming environment that fosters social interaction

- An opportunity to explore your feelings and behavior

- Increased body awareness and motor skill improvement

- Increased relaxation due to positive stress relief

- Speech practice

The theater may not be for everyone, but many have found it to be very helpful. Like many things, it depends on finding the right program. If you don't like a particular program, or teacher, you can always try a different one. In addition, there are now programs particularly targeted for the needs of adults with autism. As an example, see Shenanigans *(www.shenanigansimprov.com)*, based in Atlanta, or The Miracle Project in California (*www.themiracle project.org/*).

Reading

One way many people on the spectrum learn what to expect from others is to read about human behavior. While many people focus on the struggles those like us have with relating to others, the fact is that many people who are not on the spectrum have struggles in these areas as well. Because of this, there are many books on how to relate to others successfully.

It may seem boring to read some of these books, or you may want to spend more time reading about something that interests you more, but I have always looked at it this way: In most things we need to accomplish in life, we will need other people. There are few activities and professions in life that are completely isolated. If you want to be able to accomplish your goals, you will need to know some basics of how to interact with other people.

There are books on body language, idioms, on relationships and gender—just about any area of the social experience you can think of. Reading these books can help you to build a baseline of understanding of how people typically communicate or relate to each other, and what things mean. (Although it is important to note general trends in how people relate to one another, there will be differences in real life interactions.)

There are many books out there, but here are a few that I, or others on the spectrum, have found helpful:

- *Body Language*, by Julius Fast—a basic primer on reading body language

- *Talking from 9 to 5: Women and Men at Work*; *You just Don't Understand!*; *That's Not What I Meant!: How Conversational Style Makes or Breaks Relationships*; and *The Argument Culture: Stopping America's War of Words*, by Deborah Tannen—great books that help with understanding the social aspects of language

- *Verbal Judo: The Gentle Art of Persuasion*, by George Thompson —provides strategies for effectively communicating with others

- *Crucial Conversations: Tools for Talking When Stakes Are High*, by Kerry Patterson, Joseph Grenny, Ron McMillan, Al Switzler— provides scripts for critical conversations that you might encounter in everyday life

- *How to Win Friends and Influence People*, by Dale Carnegie—a general advice book on building relationships with others

- *The Credibility Code: How to Project Confidence and Competence When It Matters Most*, by Cara Hale Alter—provides step-by-step instructions and online videos on how to appear confident to others

- *The Five Love Languages: The Secret to Love That Lasts*, by Gary Chapman—covers the different ways we can express love to others, and how to figure out the ways that are most effective for those in our lives

- *One Minute Manners: Quick Solutions to the Most Awkward Situations You'll Ever Face at Work*, by Ann Marie Sabath

- *Emily Post's Etiquette: Manners for a New World*, by Peggy Post, Anna Post, Lizzie Post and Daniel Post Senning—a guide to common social rules

When in Doubt, Ask!

While there are a number of ways (some of which we discussed previously) that we can increase our awareness of the common patterns in how most people relate, it's unlikely you'll become an expert immediately. That's okay. Again, it's similar to learning the norms of another language or culture. You can become proficient in a language, but you may always think in your first language.

It's important to remember that it's likely you will make mistakes. There is no perfect technique that's going to teach you every little nuance. In those times it's important to ask questions. When you're around people who know you, ask them for feedback on how you are doing in the social situation. Or, if you're stuck, have someone you can pull aside and ask for guidance in a specific situation.

If you are in a situation where it's inappropriate to ask questions verbally, you might surreptitiously text a question to a trusted companion. This, of course, depends on the type of situation you are in. There are some situations where texting or being on your phone is not appropriate and would be considered rude. Figuring out which one of the situations you are in may depend on some of what you've learned by following some of the strategies discussed earlier in this chapter.

As another resource, you can turn to some of the great books that have been put together by people on the spectrum on the topic of unwritten social rules. Two good books in this category are by Judy Endow, MSW, and by Dr. Temple Grandin and Sean Barron. Judy's book is called *Learning the Hidden Curriculum: The Odyssey of One Autistic Adult* and discusses her struggles with the unwritten rules of social interactions. In it, she provides a great listing of the rules that she's been able to distill from her experiences. Sean and Temple's book is also excellent, and is called *The Unwritten Rules of Social Relationships: Decoding Social Mysteries Through the Unique Perspectives of Autism*. If you find that you frequently run into situations where you feel like you make social missteps, these books are a good place to start in terms of figuring out what some of these rules are.

Assessing Gaps and Developing Strategies to Address Them

To find your place in this world, you'll have to take all that you've learned in the processes that we have discussed in this chapter and figure out how to put them all together into a life that works for you. This will involve looking at what you're good at, what you struggle with, and how those fit with the expectations of the people you care about. I say "the people you care about," because there'll be times when you can't please everyone.

One of the very important skills you'll need to build is how to decide who and what takes priority in your life. That will depend on your own feelings, experiences, and values. What's most important to you? Is it family? Is it contributing to the greater world? Is it helping others? Is it friendship? Is it being able to work in your area of interest? Figuring out how these things rank in importance for you will help you to make the best decisions for you.

You may find that when you rank these things, those priorities may change depending on the area of life you're talking about. For example, in the workplace, meeting your boss's expectations will likely be very high on the list. However, there are also times in which you will probably have to make some tough decisions regarding whether to please a boss, or whether to please yourself or someone you care about.

When processing those kinds of decisions, it will be important to weigh the impact of your decisions on your priorities in life. If a boss asks you to do something dishonest or illegal, you'll have to look at the possible impacts on yourself. Are you comfortable doing something that's against your moral code? Will following that instruction result in criminal prosecution? If being honest and law-abiding is high on your priority list, then you may need to say no. That is okay.

One of the great things about being an adult is the fact that you get to choose what you want out of life. That will be pivotal for you in deciding your strategies for addressing gaps, because your strategies will largely depend on your own goals. When viewed through the lens of your goals, some things that others may look at as gaps may not be. It all depends on how important it is to reaching your goal.

Later in this book we will look at specific areas in life where you will need specific skill sets, like those needed for relationships and employment. In these areas we will talk about the type of skills you need and how to break them down into steps to address them in appropriate ways. In some cases, it will mean learning new skills. In other cases, it will mean choosing a different approach.

In other areas, you may need to seek help with a particular skill set. For example, if you have challenges with organization, you may ask a friend who is particularly good with organization to help you organize your home. You may ask a friend for strategies regarding how to manage your workspace or any other area where you might need help organizing information or your physical environment. You can then, in turn, help your friend in areas where he struggles. This is why understanding yourself, what you're good at, and what is more challenging can really help you.

Learning How to Challenge Yourself, Yet Set Your Own Pace

Growing as a person is a huge part of life. However, for those of us whose brains are wired a little bit differently, it can be tempting to push ourselves too far. You may experience a lot of pressure to conform to the norms of society. There are situations where conforming is appropriate or at the very least necessary, such as when personal safety is an issue. But there are times when people may expect you to "act neurotypical," for its own sake. It will be up to you to identify when this is happening and to set appropriate boundaries with others.

IN OUR OWN WORDS

If we are to do something against our neurology, it doesn't mean we can't do it, but it does mean we need practice in it, we need to recognize that we may not ever be as good at it as other people through no fault of our own, and we need to recognize that the harder we have to work, the more rest we need from it [as well]. —David Cameron Staples

At various times in your life, you'll be faced with the question of whether to improve skills in a certain area—which may involve some struggle—or whether to make peace with your limits in that area. As discussed earlier, this will often depend upon the goals you have set for yourself. There will also be other times when you'll need to decide how quickly you feel you can make a change. Only you can decide when you feel ready.

A very important component of this will be the self-awareness you build through the techniques discussed earlier in the chapter. You'll need to be able to identify when stress is reaching a crisis point for you and take appropriate action to prevent a problem. This may involve setting boundaries with others.

Just as we're driven to always learn something new, to always get better in our areas of expertise and our special interests, it's always been my experience that we need to do that in the rest of our lives as well. In a well-lived life, there is always tension between where you are and where you plan to be. Be sure that the path you take is one *you* choose.

POINTS TO REMEMBER

- Self-advocacy is a crucial skill for those of us on the spectrum.

- Self-awareness can be built and in a number of ways, such as: mindfulness practices, asking yourself questions, and seeking the input of others.

- Alexithymia and sensory issues can make self-awareness difficult.

- In order to be effective in self-advocacy, you will need to set priorities regarding your goals and values in life.

- When choosing how to address gaps between your abilities and the expectations of others, you will need to make strategic choices based on these goals and values.

- Goals and priorities may be different depending on the area of life in question, such as your personal life and your professional life.

- If the expectations of others clash with your values, it's okay to say no.

- Sometimes, the solution for a gap in skills or abilities may be partnering up with someone who has a profile of skills and abilities that complements yours.

- It's important to use self-awareness skills to identify when your stress levels are getting too high and to take appropriate action.

- In order to grow, there should always be a tension between what you want to accomplish and what you have accomplished.

CHAPTER 2

Managing Emotional and Sensory Issues

Sensory challenges and emotions can be deeply intertwined, and they can cause a lot of pain and discomfort for those of us on the spectrum. Making large transitions in life can be stressful. It will be important for you to learn how to effectively manage your emotions to prevent difficult situations from happening.

In this chapter, we will discuss some of the ways in which you can identify emotion and sensory sensations. In addition, we will talk about how to handle the anxiety, worry, and stress that they can cause. We will discuss some ways to minimize this kind of stress.

Finally, we will discuss some ways to express emotions, especially problematic ones, in appropriate ways. Ideally, we would want to prevent issues that can trigger unwanted emotions from occurring, but in the real world they sometimes do. When this happens, it will be important to understand how to recover from them for the sake of yourself and others.

Sensory Issues Can Have Social Implications

I love rock 'n' roll, but for almost a whole year, I could barely stand to listen to it. I didn't know why. I spent most of my afternoons locked away in my bedroom listening to classical music or NPR, because it was all I could tolerate.

My mother became very concerned at my withdrawal. She would burst into my room and talk to me, to try to get me to engage. This put us at odds, because I was desperate to withdraw. But I couldn't explain to anyone what I was feeling.

I only knew that my nerves felt stretched. I was in pain. Every few months or so, the tension would build up and I would explode. I would yell and scream, feeling totally out of control. In later years my mother and I would discuss it; she'd say, "It seemed like you didn't even know what you were angry about. I thought it was just teenage angst."

I now know that it had a lot to do with stress, anxiety, and sensory issues. During a typical school day, I would become nervous and stressed. I would worry about my grades. Then I would worry about getting my work done. I set goals for myself that were way too ambitious, which I struggled to reach. As the pressure built, the stress would cause my sensory sensitivities to be extremely heightened.

When I was in that state, the world became excruciating. I'd jump at every sound. My muscles would clench every time someone talked to me. So I withdrew in a desperate attempt to calm a nervous system that was on painfully high alert. Then one day, my mother would say or do something, and it would trigger a massive meltdown.

Part of the reason I would get so angry was that I assumed that my mother knew the amount of pain I was in and just went about her business anyway. I thought she just didn't care. One day not long ago, we were reminiscing when I asked, "Do you remember that year when I couldn't listen to music?" My mother said, "No, not really."

That's when I realized the truth. All those times when my mother's attempts at engagement triggered a meltdown, she wasn't being insensitive or ignoring my pain. She didn't know it existed. *Because I never told her, and she had no other way of knowing.*

Who would have thought that sensory issues could cause such a misunderstanding? Certainly not me. This is how I learned the cost of not being aware of my emotional makeup, and the importance of building skills to overcome these challenges.

Recognizing Emotion and Sensory Input

As discussed in the previous chapter, those of us on the spectrum can sometimes have problems recognizing emotion. This can also be true of sensory input. In both cases this can be problematic, because this means you may find yourself overloading in either of these realms before you even realize there's an issue.

So what are some ways that you can work to better identify when you are becoming overwhelmed by emotional or sensory stimuli?

Mindfulness Practices and Visualization

In a lot of ways, some of the mindfulness practices that we talked about in the first chapter can be helpful in this regard. Learning to quiet down your mind and to sit quietly and observe what you feel in your body can make it easier to identify what those feelings are. When you sit down and focus on what's going on in your body and your brain in a specific moment, you find that there is a lot of "noise." If you can reduce that noise, then it means there's less stimulation/input to sort through.

One approach toward mindfulness was particularly useful to me in these types of situations. That was visualization. Because I am a visual thinker, like many people on the spectrum, it helped me a great deal to visualize abstract concepts, such as emotions, in more easily accessible ways, using metaphor.

In Our Own Words

I experience my AS less as an inability to process stimuli than as a need to process them in slow motion, and, underlying that, an inability to do so intuitively, forcing me to rely upon reflection and the drawing of relevant analogies that help me to make sense of things. —Jack

When I was a teen, I had a deep interest in historical epochs such as the medieval times. So, I used this interest. When I got stuck, I'd imagine that my emotions were people in a medieval walled city. Why would people barricade themselves inside a walled city? If they're completely under siege. What is the cost of that? Well, they might be safe from invaders, but they would also be cut off from sources of food and water, etc.

Aided by this metaphor, I began to realize that the reason I was not feeling emotion wasn't because it didn't exist but because my neurology was feeling under attack. It had walled off my emotions as a form of protection. I realized, too, that if I didn't figure out how to fight off the attack, the townspeople—barricaded without food or water inside the city walls—would eventually die or try to break out violently. This helped me to process these abstract emotions and figure out how to address them.

This metaphor may not resonate with you, but you might find other metaphors that do. If you are a person who finds it easier to deal with less abstract concepts, it may help to try to find some metaphors that work for you, such as concepts related to a special interest.

Try to Put It Into Words

For some of us, putting into words what we're feeling can be helpful. This can mean talking about this feeling with another person. It could mean writing about it. Or, if you have no one to talk to, it could even be talking through it out loud to yourself (although you'd probably want to wait until you are alone to do this).

If you are a person who likes to write, it may help to keep a journal. When you feel something you're not sure about, you can sit down and write about it. This will also allow you to go back to the feeling later if you need to. Sometimes you won't figure out what the feeling means right away. It might take time.

If writing things by hand is uncomfortable for you, or just doesn't flow easily, another option would be keeping a blog, or just keeping a journal in a Word document or some other electronic form. Although many blogs are public, you can also restrict a blog to only friends, family, or even just yourself. Having your writing online gives you the freedom to use that journal to work something out even when you're not in front of your home computer.

Identify Patterns

One way of building awareness of problematic emotions and sensory issues is observing your own past in order to identify common patterns leading up to a crisis. This is especially important for those who have alexithymia, because you may not recognize the warning signs of a crisis until they're too intense to overcome. You may feel your emotions go from zero to sixty in a second. In those situations, it might appear that you're upset over nothing, when actually the tension has been building for some time. So it's a good idea to identify secondary indicators that commonly precede a crisis due to emotional or sensory overload.

One of the adults I interviewed compared these secondary indicators to strange noises an engine might make before the check engine light comes on, an analogy used by a fellow member of a support group. These "strange engine noises" are different for each person—for some it may mean a change in voice volume or tone (whiny or more monotone), others may notice changes in their breathing, still others will stim, or feel odd sensations in their body. If you can identify your "strange engine noises," this will help you a great deal to realize when you may be nearing the point of being overwhelmed.

Ennien Ashbrook describes the best way to identify one's own "strange engine noises": ". . . Remember an incident, and think back on how you were feeling [leading] up to it. When you think back on several incidents, usually you can start to recognize patterns in your behavior that can provide you with clues on when to head things off."

Time

In some cases the best technique for understanding emotion is to just give yourself time. What you can't make sense of in the moment, because of stress or being overwhelmed, you may make sense of later. Many adults on the spectrum find that just giving it time helps a great deal.

The important thing, when you decide to give it time, is not to feel bad about yourself because you need this time. If you're someone who has trouble making sense of your own emotions, that's how you're built and that's okay. You just need to find the best way to work with the fact that you need more time to process your emotions than others do.

Dealing with Anxiety and Worry

Anxiety and worry can be a particular problem for those of us on the spectrum. Anxiety can intensify when anticipating a social situation. There are certain thinking styles that those of us on the spectrum have that may make it difficult to break out of this cycle of anxiety or worry.

When it comes to anxiety and worry, you can approach it in several ways. You can approach it from a cognitive standpoint—in other words, what you're thinking. You can approach it from a physical standpoint; for example, dealing with the sensory feelings of tension and stress in the body. You can also address it with action.

Thinking about Your Thoughts

There are a number of "thought traps" that you can fall into that may create worry and anxiety. So, when you recognize that you are feeling anxiety or worry, you'll want to think about what you are thinking about. This will help you to identify if there are destructive thought patterns at work.

Some common destructive thought patterns are: black or white thinking, "should" thoughts, "catastrophizing," personalization, over-generalizing and name-calling, focusing on the negative, and relying too much on your emotions. Each one of these patterns requires a different approach. What they have in common is that they tend to cause you to see the situation in a way that isn't really true.

Thinking in Black or White

When it comes to black-and-white thinking, one of the first things that helps us is just becoming aware that you do it. Black-and-white thinking is binary, yes or no, right or wrong. There are some situations in which this may be appropriate, especially in certain fields, such as engineering or computer science. However, when it comes to social thinking it can be counterproductive.

For me, learning to work with this particular trait has been recognizing what it means to me in daily life. There are some situations in which it is extremely useful. It helps me to "get" computers and computer logic, and sometimes helps me to see things in a way other people don't.

IN OUR OWN WORDS

You don't need to respond to your first impulse. Sometimes, maybe even most times, that is wrong. Give your cognition time to catch up. It's hard to fight your impulses, but often that is the best thing to do. Pause and reflect. It is more satisfying.
—Michael F. Wilcox, Autistic Adult

But this type of thinking can cause difficulties when trying to figure out a social situation, because you may ask multiple people what is right and what is wrong in a specific situation and you will get many different answers.

When you receive conflicting advice, try to resolve this conflict by looking at all the salient facts of the situation and making a decision about what you believe based on your perceptions and the knowledge that you have. Each person has his own set of beliefs and perceptions that will impact what he believes to be the truth. If your own beliefs depend on your own neurological makeup and your very specific set of knowledge and experiences, it really doesn't make sense that anyone else would ever think exactly as you do. That's a good thing, because nobody else brings to the world exactly that which you bring.

Should Thoughts

Closely related to black-and-white thinking is getting caught in "should" thoughts. Should thoughts are thoughts that reflect dissatisfaction with the reality of what is. You may find yourself focusing on the things that people shouldn't do, or the things that shouldn't have been, or the way the world shouldn't be.

When directed toward yourself, this often becomes negative self-talk that is self-defeating. When you find yourself thinking these types of thoughts, challenge those thoughts by asking, "Who said that I was supposed to be this way?" Then follow up with the question, "Do I agree with those people?" If the answer is that you don't agree with those negative messages, you have the choice not to believe them.

If the answer to that question is that you do agree with this statement, the second question to ask yourself is, "Is that a reasonable expectation?" For example, if you're five feet tall, and you think you should be five foot seven, that is an aspect of yourself you can't change. The expectation is unreasonable and futile, so it isn't worth spending much time worrying about.

If it is a reasonable expectation, and you simply failed to meet that expectation of yourself, ask, "What can I do to make sure that I do better in this area in the future?" This translates the worry into a concrete action that you can take. So instead of looping on a thought like, "I should be more organized," you can translate the energy you would have spent worrying about the past into working on your organizational skills.

Overgeneralizing and Name-Calling

Another thought pattern that often follows "should" thoughts and/or black-and-white thinking is a pair of patterns that I call overgeneralization and name-calling. In these patterns, what happens is you recognize something—maybe a "should" thought—then you draw from that a generalization. "I really hurt Jane with that stupid statement I made. I really should be more sensitive. I'm such a jerk!"

When you catch yourself having these kinds of thoughts, you can use the techniques we talked about regarding "should" thoughts, but then you would also want to look at the second half of the statement. When you call yourself a name, it's often an indicator that you're overgeneralizing. Are you really a jerk? Would a real jerk even care that he hurt Jane's feelings?

In many of these situations, if you look at it logically, with all the facts, you realize that the statement you just made isn't really the truth. In most cases when you're calling yourself a name (or when you're calling someone else a name) the reality is that you are a person who behaved in an insensitive way, but that doesn't necessarily make you a jerk.

What's most challenging about this particular thought pattern is that it gets in the way of your reaching your goals. If you say, "I'm a jerk!" it doesn't really lead to constructive ways of dealing with the issue. In this case, a better solution would be to ask yourself a more useful question.

Instead of calling yourself a jerk, you may want to consider asking yourself questions such as:

- "What did I do to hurt Jane's feelings?" —This identifies what *not* to do next time.

- "Why did I say it?" —This question addresses motivation. Was it a mistake? Were you angry? Maybe jealous? The answers to these questions will impact how you approach changing your future behavior.

- "What can I do differently so that I don't hurt Jane's feelings next time?" —This question focuses on what you can proactively do to prevent the outcome that's causing your anxiety.

When it comes to these styles of thinking, it's important to recognize that you can't change the past. You can't change what you've done or the mistakes you've made, but you can work to prevent such mistakes in the future and to work to make amends, if appropriate.

Catastrophizing

"Catastrophizing" is a particular type of overgeneralization having to do with consequences. When you're catastrophizing, you overestimate the consequences of a particular mistake or event. For example, you may find yourself thinking: "I misunderstood my boss's instructions regarding this task. He's going to think I'm stupid and fire me."

When you recognize this type of pattern, the first thing to do is, again, ask yourself a few questions. First, ask whether this is really true. Is this task so important that this one mistake will result in his firing you? Are there other things that you've done really well that would balance out this mistake?

The next question to ask yourself is whether this consequence is as bad as you might think. Do you like the job? Is it a job at which you really want to stay? If not, then it might not be such a bad thing.

When I am particularly caught up in this type of mindset, I ask myself two particular questions. I ask, "One hundred years from now, will anyone remember or care about this event or mistake?"

And, "If I were trapped alone on a tropical island miles from any-one else, would this matter?"

In today's hyperindustrialized world full of computers and noise, we tend to forget that the very basics of what we need to survive has very little to do with people's thoughts and expecta-tions of us. It has to do with food, water, and a safe place to sleep. If we have these things, we are actually doing pretty well. It helps from time to time to remind ourselves of that.

Personalization and Being a "Mind Reader"

Another thought trap you might find yourself falling into is personalization—when you assume you're responsible for others' negative feelings. It can be easy to fall into this, because we find so many times that people are angry with us without our knowledge. Those who expect you to just figure out their feelings can be very mean if you don't.

Many of us start to protect ourselves by making the default assumption that if someone is acting differently or potentially upset that it must mean she *is* upset and that she is upset with something *we* did. The problem with this is that there are many cases in which this is not true, and these assumptions only stand in the way of truly understanding or helping the person or in simply making a connection with that person. Unfortunately, it can also make people think that you are egotistical or self-centered, that you think everything is about you.

The reality is usually not that you want it to be about you, but that you *fear* that it is about you and don't know what to do about it. The problem with assuming this is that it puts you in a position where you are extremely anxious, and you're unlikely to be able to take concrete action to deal with the issue at hand. It also assumes that you were able to read her mind, which isn't true. It may be that she is stressed for other reasons. It may be that she is feeling bad about herself. You can't know unless you ask.

So when you recognize yourself starting to have thoughts like, "Jerry just walked by, but he didn't say, 'Hi.' He must be mad at me," ask yourself if you know for a fact that that's true. Is it possible that something else is going on? The answer is usually yes. Jerry might've just gotten some bad news about a family member. He may be focused and just didn't see you. He may have something in his eye or be mad at someone else.

It does very little good to worry about something that may not be true. If you really are worried and want to know, it's best to ask. If you feel self-conscious about asking, you can ask a more indirect question like: "You don't seem quite yourself today. Is anything wrong?" By asking an open-ended question, you give Jerry the option to tell you what's going on with him and you show him that you care. If he tells you, "I just found out my grandmother is in the hospital, and I'm really worried," then you know he wasn't upset with you, and you now have the opportunity to offer support when he really needs it. That's a win-win situation.

Focusing on the Negative

When you get discouraged, it's hard not to find your thoughts going to a negative place. As in some of the previous "thought traps," try to recognize when you're seeing things not quite as they are, and ask yourself questions to help you see the situation more clearly.

It's tempting when two or three things go wrong to look at those things and to think that everything else is wrong. The problem is that's rarely true. If you find yourself thinking absolute thoughts like, "I have no place in life," "Nobody likes me," or just, "I hate my job and my life sucks," you might ask yourself some questions about whether these things are true.

If you hate your job, does that really mean your whole life sucks? Are there other things in your life that you *do* like? What about hobbies? Your special interests? Friends? Family? If you find yourself getting upset, try to make sure that you are seeing an accurate picture of your life, not just how it "feels" in the moment.

Relying Too Much on Your Emotions

When your emotions are strong, especially when they're strong *negative* emotions, they can really color what you see about your current situation. Keep in mind that just because a situation or circumstance generates a lot of anxiety, it doesn't necessarily mean that this level of anxiety is proportionate to the actual impact of the situation.

When you feel anxiety very strongly, always stop and ask yourself questions about the real impact of the situation. If it appears that your anxiety is out of proportion to the actual circumstances, then you may want to try some of the techniques we'll go through in the next section.

In Our Own Words

Try to relax and let go of unreasonable expectations of others. Try to stay positive and not allow others to bring you down.
—Steve Summers, Adult on the Autism Spectrum

Other Ways of Reducing Anxiety

One of the problems with anxiety and worry and fear is that they are primal emotions—in mankind's early history they served as protective responses to keep us safe from harm. Unfortunately for those of us on the spectrum, many of us are hypersensitive to the types of stimuli that will trigger these feelings. Once the "fight or flight" response has been triggered, it can be hard to calm yourself.

If you find that this happens frequently, and other techniques don't reduce your stress, your doctor may prescribe medication for this. If you take this route, your doctor will need to know about your diagnosis, because many of those on the spectrum have unusual reactions to the typical drugs prescribed for conditions such as anxiety or depression. Your doctor will need to work closely with you, and may need to give you a different dose than would be appropriate for someone who is not on the autism spectrum.

Another thing you want to be aware of is the tendency that many of us have to perseverate, which means we get "stuck" on thinking about a particular topic. This can be a good thing when we're working on solving a problem, but it can be a very bad thing when it involves something anxiety provoking.

If you catch yourself perseverating over something that causes anxiety, try to do something to disrupt that cycle. Go for a walk, do yoga, or work out. Take on a project you really enjoy that will occupy your attention. Sometimes it's helpful just to call someone and talk to her about it, or even talk to her about something else. All these things can sometimes interrupt or crowd out the problematic thought pattern.

Expressing the Emotion of Being Overwhelmed Safely and Appropriately

The best weapon that I have found against being emotionally overwhelmed is identifying emotions early, as we discussed earlier in this chapter. But what do you do once you've identified those emotions?

The answer to that question will vary based on your setting and situation, and the extent of your feelings of being overwhelmed. First, remove yourself from the situation if at all possible. It'll be very difficult to calm yourself if you are still dealing with the sensory or emotional stimuli that drove you into the overload to begin with.

If there are others around, you also need to find a way to communicate to them that you are in distress and need to step away. If you are in a gathering of friends or family who know about your diagnosis, you may be able to tell them directly. It may be helpful to prepare for such a situation by having a signal that communicates distress or concern.

When deciding what your signal should be, you'll want to make sure that it is something you can easily do when you're in a state of overload. This is especially important to consider if you usually speak, but sometimes lose the ability to speak under stress. You'll want to have a signal that can work when you have no voice. In addition, you want to be clear with your friends and family what exactly you need them to do when they're given the signal.

Should they make excuses and make arrangements to leave? Or, should they just find a way to pull you aside inconspicuously so that you can find a peaceful place to calm down for a little while? By having this in place, you can communicate your distress in a way that won't make you feel conspicuous but that still communicates what you need.

Once you've been able to remove yourself from the situation, you'll need to find a way to calm your overloaded system. What works for each person will be slightly different, but it can be as simple as sitting in a quiet dark room, taking a warm bath, listening to soothing music that calms you down, or doing some sort of physical activity that gets the built-up energy out of your system.

As an adult, you want to be very careful about overloads that look like rage. If you let yourself get pushed to that level of overload, it may put you in a very difficult position in a number of situations, such as during employment, or if you are in a public place. If you let yourself get too overloaded, you may even find yourself in trouble with the law.

When I was a teen, I learned an effective technique to prevent overloads, for me. It began when I recognized that suddenly feeling emotional numbness was one of my "strange engine noises." It meant that my emotions had built to a dangerous level and would soon boil over into a meltdown. The key to preventing this was finding a safe way to express these emotions before that happened. Music was particularly evocative for me, so I learned to use this to provoke the emotional release I needed.

I put together collections of music that evoked specific feelings. I had collections that made me feel sad, and collections that made me feel happy. When I'd feel the numbness, I'd use the music to provoke myself to cry, until I felt release. This would prevent an overload that would manifest as rage. Then, to recover, I would play the music that made me feel happy. This allowed me to safely express my emotions before they got to a damaging level.

You may have different "strange engine noises." Music may not be the tool that works for you, but if you can find those things that help you release tension, and learn to recognize the signs that tell you when you need to use them, you'll be better equipped to manage your emotions.

POINTS TO REMEMBER

- Recognizing emotion can sometimes be a struggle for those of us on the spectrum.

- For visual thinkers, and those who deal better with less abstract concepts, using visual metaphor for representing emotion may help.

- Identifying secondary indicators may help detect an overload before it reaches a crisis point.

- Reducing anxiety and worry can be done through a number of methods—recognizing and defining damaging thought patterns, practicing self-soothing techniques, or through medication.

- When overload occurs, remove yourself from the source of stress as soon as possible.

- You may want to work out an emergency signal with friends and family that you can use to notify them when you're in distress and need help in dealing with it.

- If you recognize your "strange engine noises," you may be able to use provocative music or activities to express your emotion or stress before it reaches a critical point.

CHAPTER 3

Communication

Communication can be frustrating for those of us on the spectrum due to differences between our communication style and that of neurotypical people. We may misunderstand the communication of others, or they may misunderstand—or not recognize—our own attempts to communicate. In this chapter, I'll share some of what I've learned about these differences. This will include many ways in which our communication and cognitive differences can be an advantage.

We'll discuss some of the ways that we can minimize misunderstandings brought about by the way others may perceive behaviors and communication styles typical to those on the spectrum. We'll cover how to communicate about your differences, even if you decide you don't want to disclose your diagnosis. We'll also go over some tips on how to use effective listening techniques, and how to compensate for body language differences.

On Communicating Differently

In the social world, there are many different ways that information is communicated. Unfortunately for us, much communication (as much as 90 percent) is nonverbal. This is why for many of us the social world can be so confusing. Because we don't automatically learn body language in the same way or at the same rate as those not on the spectrum, this means that we miss a lot of social information being conveyed that other people recognize.

Given the emphasis that so many put on the neurotypical style of communicating, it can be easy to get overwhelmed or discouraged at the differences in how we process social communication. But it's important to remember that there wouldn't be a thriving self-help industry if the neurotypical style of communication were perfect—those with a neurotypical makeup have misunderstandings, too. The reality is that all people struggle with communication to some degree. Some people who are considered great communicators in the public square may not be good at communication in certain contexts, such as within their personal relationships.

On the other hand, there are people who would struggle, or even find it nearly impossible, to speak to even a small group of people who went on to accomplish great things. Mahatma Gandhi, who became an influential world leader, struggled a great deal in the early years with speaking at all. In his autobiography, he wrote, "It was impossible for me to speak *impromptu*. I hesitated whenever I had to face strange audiences and avoided making a speech whenever I could. Even today I do not think I could or would even be inclined to keep a meeting of friends engaged in idle talk." He went on to call this hesitancy of speech, which once annoyed him, "a pleasure." His reasoning? "A man of few words will rarely be thoughtless in his speech; he will measure every word."

If you look across the autism community, what you'll find is that there are many people who communicate differently who are very successful and inspiring people. There are the people you will meet in this book. There are people like Temple Grandin, who did not speak until much later than her peers. Or people like Sharisa Joy Kochmeister, Tracy Thresher, Larry Bissonnette, and Carly Fleischmann, who communicate brilliantly by typing, who present at conferences, are profiled on TV, and in movies. Navigating a world that communicates differently from you can be very challenging, but it doesn't mean that you can't be successful. It just means that you may need to do some things differently.

What I have found is much like what Gandhi described. Knowing that my communication style is different has forced me to be more conscious regarding how I communicate. That is a strength. As you go out into the world, you may find any number of unexpected strengths in areas others may call deficits. To me, finding these is part of the great adventure that is life.

Differences Between Autistic and Non-Autistic Thinking Styles

One thing that observing has taught me (and the research has confirmed) is that there are distinct differences in communication styles between those on the autism spectrum and those who are not, and that extends to our thinking as well. As with many traits that are common to those on the autism spectrum, these differences can be both a strength and a challenge, depending on their context.

One very key difference is how we go about solving problems. Research confirms that the typical bias for those on the autism spectrum is to focus on details first. This can be a great asset in situations where detail is crucial, but it can make certain situations difficult especially when it comes to communication. Because regardless of what form the communication takes, when you're speaking to someone whose bias is for the big picture or the integrated whole, this can lead to miscommunications and/or devaluing the input of the other person. In the adult world, what you'll find is that there are needs for both types of thinking. But sometimes people identify so strongly with their own way of thinking that they can't appreciate the style of another.

In Our Own Words

People tell me that I think out of the box, and that I see situations and developments in my field of work a lot faster than others. Also, my way of approaching problems differs from others. I don't really see a need to adjust, other than taking more time to explain. But, people are not always used to my way of approaching problems—I learned to take time so that others can learn about my typical approaches. —Peter, Adult on the Autism Spectrum, works in the financial industry

One particularly crucial skill for getting along in the world will be to build a tolerance for thinking styles that are different from yours. In fact, there are many times in life when you will likely want to partner with someone whose profile of skills and abilities is complementary to yours. If you can develop mutual respect for each person's way of thinking, and an appreciation for the situations in which each is effective, it will be very helpful to being successful in the world. Many of my most successful professional partnerships are with people who are not on the spectrum and whose strengths are the opposite of mine.

Watching some of these colleagues, I see that communication is often used as a way to connect to another person, rather than as a means to convey vital information. That can be very frustrating for some of us, because on the surface, this kind of communication can seem superficial, or even pointless. I feel more connected to a person if she speaks to me about something that has substance, something I care about. But when I'm speaking to someone who values "small talk" as a way of connecting, I try to oblige.

I look at this as simply "speaking to them in their language." As you build relationships with other people, if they're the right people, they will learn to reciprocate and "speak your language."

I've learned to make statements like, "I tend to be more detail focused so it would really help me if you would be very specific in explaining what you want me to do." This allows me to communicate that my style is different, which changes how they perceive some of my behavior and reactions. It also tells them how they could interact with me to get the best result. Another form of this, popularized by Dr. Tony Attwood, is using the framework, "I'm the kind of person who ..." For example, you would say, "I'm the kind of person who is overwhelmed by lots of sound and noise. So, wearing headphones as I work helps me to focus."

Using this type of communication is often appropriate in situations where full disclosure would be uncomfortable or the person you're speaking to simply wouldn't understand enough to understand how to accommodate your needs. Once you've used these types of techniques enough times, people start to get an idea of what "your language" is. If they are the type of person who values reciprocity in a relationship, they will usually begin to meet you halfway. If they are a person who doesn't value differences, then they are likely someone with whom a deeper relationship would not really be feasible or, dare I say it, desirable.

Another aspect that's very important is learning how to manage other people's expectations in areas where they are different from you. For example, if you're working with someone who is very social and finds social interactions very easy, it may not occur to him initially to realize that the same is not true for you. In fact, if he finds social interaction energizing, he may be driven to seek it. Because of this, he may not understand why you would withdraw if you find yourself getting overloaded by social interaction.

Since he doesn't realize that it's draining for you, he may think your withdrawal has something to do with your feelings about him and therefore take it personally. You can prevent this by saying something like, "I am a person who really likes people; however, sometimes interaction can be draining for me. So, if I withdraw for a while, please don't take it personally." This way you can prevent misunderstandings from the beginning, instead of having to repair an interaction after the fact.

In Our Own Words

There's also expectation management. I like to call this problem that of being punished for success. People expect that because you can do this thing, that you can do it indefinitely and just like they can. —David Cameron Staples

Another difference in communication styles between those who are on the spectrum and those who are not is in the area of emotion. As discussed previously, some of us can have trouble identifying emotion to begin with. This can make it difficult to communicate your feelings, so you may be tempted not to talk about them, but rather stick to topics that are more factual or logical in nature. There's nothing wrong with that, but some may judge it as odd. In a work situation, this is probably okay, as the bias in the workplace tends to be toward discussing business, with the exception of communication that happens as part of social ritual, such as "small talk."

A particular difference in thinking I have observed is in how those with a neurotypical makeup and people with autism process social situations that relate to emotion. Once I was riding in the car with my husband. He had received a call from someone raising a concern about one of his employees. He assured the caller he would reprimand the employee, hung up, and then called the employee. He had a discussion with the employee in which he identified what the employee did wrong, talked to the employee about the behavior, and gave direction as to what to do better next time. All in all, however, I would not have classified it in my own mind as a reprimand, at least not a severe one. I didn't hear anger, or an aggressive tone, which is what I assumed the first caller had wanted.

He then called the first caller and told that person about the reprimand. When he finally hung up I was a bit confused. Although I recognized he had given the employee correction, it did not seem as severe as was warranted based on the misstep of the employee. So I asked him about it. In the past, before we were aware that I was on the spectrum, he would see such a question as criticism or accusation, but now he knows it's simply a straightforward question based on a genuine desire to understand.

It turned out that the difference in our perceptions of the situation was based on differences in how we were measuring the severity of the reprimand. He explained to me that the employee was a new one, that he was nervous and eager to please, and was still in the trial period, so he was still not fully secure in the status of his job. He explained that he was intentionally mild in how he delivered the reprimand because the employee's own anxieties would amplify the impact of the reprimand.

He was judging the severity of the reprimand based on how it would be *received* by the employee. Without any knowledge of the social cues and situation that my husband was reading automatically, I was judging the reprimand based on my perception of the words and tone in which he said them. We were talking about the same concept but using different definitions. This is something I see in communications of all types, not just those between people who are on the spectrum and those who are not. And that is why it's important to understand the differences and try to figure out how those differences may impact how your words and communications are received.

Developing Clarity in Communication

What some of the techniques discussed in the previous section teach us is that we have control over *how* we communicate, and we don't need to be limited to the status quo. In other words, we can consciously structure our own communication in ways that make it more successful. In order to do this we need to think about precisely what we want other people to hear.

Many people, on the spectrum or not, make the mistake of assuming they know what another person wants or needs, and about what that person understands about their own needs. Making assumptions has led many people to serious breakdowns in their own relationships because they overestimated that accuracy of their ability to read body language and identify the needs of others. As a result, there is a large industry designed around helping people relate their feelings and needs more explicitly.

Those of us on the spectrum actually have an advantage in this area. We know that we need to confirm our understanding of social cues and body language, and so we're less likely to make assumptions. What you will learn is that there is nothing wrong with clearly stating what your wants and needs are. In fact, it's often crucial to getting what you need. You don't get what you don't ask for.

Because of how I process details, I have learned to be very methodical in how I communicate things. I also ask for the same in return. For example, I know that my way of solving problems is often somewhat different than that of my bosses, so when I'm given a task or project I will ask for the direction in the format that I need it. What I learned to do was to say, "I have a different way of thinking than a lot of other people, and that means I go about solving problems a little bit differently. If you could tell me exactly what you want to accomplish, I'll figure out how to get there. If I have questions, I will let you know." This gave the person giving me the task the opportunity to explain what exactly she was trying to do, and gave me the opportunity to use my creativity and skills to accomplish it in a way that worked for me. And, because the people who hired me often hired me precisely because I had a different skill set than they did, it provided me the opportunity to come up with a new and innovative way of carrying out something that they might not have thought about.

Understanding what you need is the first step; the second step is communicating that need. Sometimes it means breaking down your needs into smaller chunks, and communicating them step-by-step. When doing that, it's helpful to stop and solicit feedback from the other person. A useful, all-purpose question for this is, "Does that make sense?" If she says no, then you can clarify with an answer like, "Here is my reasoning behind that." Then you can follow up to make sure that she understands.

In Our Own Words

I try to cut up the thing that I want to communicate in bits that I can explain step-by-step. The payoff is tangible: I became a university associate professor. —Peter

The Importance of Being a Good Listener

It's also very important to pay attention to the quality of your listening skills. Basic to this is making sure that you can hear others in the first place. If you're like me, and background noise clashes with your ability to understand someone, it's a good idea to take measures like asking to move to a quieter area. You can say something like, "I'm sorry. The background noise here is very loud, and it's making it very difficult for me to hear you. I really want to make sure that I hear what you have to say. Could we have this conversation some place that's a little bit quieter?" This tells them that you're paying attention, are interested in what they're saying, and helps them to understand why you might seem distracted.

When it comes to listening, it's also important to pay attention to the *way* in which you listen. We tend to think of hearing and listening as the same thing, but they are not. Hearing is something you can do by accident. Listening is an active state. When you're truly listening, you give your full attention to what the person is saying. While another person is talking, many of us have the tendency to allocate most of our attention to thinking about what we want to say next, thinking about something unrelated, or just waiting to talk. This isn't the best way to listen.

Equally important to listening is communicating that we are listening. We can be listening intently, but people may still get frustrated with us if we don't *communicate* that we are doing so. Among those with a neurotypical makeup, the typical way to communicate that we are listening is via eye contact, paired with leaning slightly toward the person. If you find eye contact difficult, then you may want to communicate your attention in a different way. For many people on the spectrum, making eye contact is doable but very distracting and thus makes it harder to listen. For others it is simply painful, which is not conducive to true listening.

If you find it less distracting to look at someone's forehead or elsewhere near a person's face, you may want to do that. Otherwise, you might want to say something like, "I am really interested in what you are saying, but it makes it easier for me to understand you if I put all my attention on what I'm hearing, so I may look down." Because of auditory processing issues, some of us tend to focus on the speaker's mouth in order to supplement what we hear by reading lips. If that is something that you do, explain what you are doing. This way the person knows that you're listening and that you're not meeting her eyes because you are trying to understand her in the best way possible.

Another good practice for listening well is to recap what a person has said to confirm that you understanding him correctly. To do this, you can say something like, "So, just to make sure I understand what you're saying, let me recap. What you're saying is . . ." When I do this, I often paraphrase, or say what he said in a slightly different way, which shows him that you're not just repeating his words, but that you understand his meaning.

If you know the other person often uses a particular term differently than you do, don't use that word in your recap. Use your own interpretation. This will ensure that they clearly understand what you are trying to communicate. If your understanding is *not* correct, then the person will often say, "No, that's not really what I meant. What I meant to say was . . ." If the disagreement was only in how you characterized a particular word or phrase he used, then he may say something like, "Yes, that's what I meant, but what I meant by _____, was . . ."

In Our Own Words

We need to find a way to comfortably talk to each other and tell each other what's true for us and what we really need. —Brian R. King

Because it takes longer for us to process speech, you may need to plan how to handle gaps or delays in conversation. If there is a long delay after the person has spoken in which you don't respond, she may think that you're not paying attention. Because of this, it's a good idea to have a few standard phrases or gestures to use to communicate to the speaker that you are listening and that you plan to respond but that you need some time to process what she said and respond appropriately.

You might put up your index finger, with your palm facing them, and say something like, "Could you give me a moment? I need a couple of seconds to process what you've said." If you consistently use this statement and gesture together, eventually people will recognize that's how you communicate. There may come a time when you may not need to say the words. In American body language, this often means, "One moment," or "One second," so sometimes this gesture itself will send the message on its own.

However you communicate, whether it's via voice, picture, or computer, you don't have to let the other person drive the interaction. You can choose your own words and communication style in order to drive the rhythm and direction of the conversation. It's important to realize that you do have some control.

POINTS TO REMEMBER

- Everyone struggles, to some degree, to communicate well.

- Knowing that you communicate differently can be a strength, because you don't make unwarranted assumptions.

- People on the autism spectrum often have different styles of thinking and solving problems than those not on the spectrum.

- One very important skill for being successful is learning to value and understand the different communication and thinking styles of others.

- You can help others to understand your needs by using, "I tend to be . . ." or "I'm the kind of person who . . ." statements to communicate your differences and needs.

- Listening is different from hearing. Listening is an active process.

- It's a good idea to recap what a person says to you to ensure you have clearly understood what was said.

- However you communicate, you don't have to let the other person drive the interaction. You can choose how to direct the conversation.

CHAPTER 4

Safety

Safety is a concern for any adult, but for people on the autism spectrum, it can be even more so. Differences in sensory processing, body language, communication, social skills, and a number of other factors can cause additional challenges. In this chapter, we will go over some of these issues and strategies for addressing them. You will learn the basic practices for keeping to some simple "rules of the road" for staying safe as you become more independent.

You will learn how to identify and seek out safe places. Understanding how to assess the safety of a particular environment is a crucial skill for keeping yourself safe when you're out and about, and for other life skills, like choosing a place to live. For us, people can be particularly difficult to understand, but in this interdependent world, it's important to learn to interact with them. We'll discuss some skills for success, including knowing how, when, and why to say no.

The neurological differences that come along with being on the autism spectrum can also impact your physical safety. Learning to navigate through challenges like sensory processing issues, differences in motor control, and attention are very important for keeping yourself safe. In this chapter, you will learn how to protect yourself physically, as well as mentally and emotionally.

One day, when I was about nineteen, my stepmother showed up on my doorstep unexpectedly. "When are you going to move out of this dump?" she demanded.

Angry and upset at being hassled, I yelled at her, defied her, and told her to go away. I didn't understand that she was afraid, with good reason.

The apartment I had chosen for myself a few weeks before was a small efficiency in an older building, with a very reasonable rent. What I didn't realize—was in fact oblivious to—was that it was in a less than desirable neighborhood. When I had visited, I focused on the "quaint" old historical row houses that surrounded it and the pretty tile bathroom with a built-in dressing area.

I was walking home one afternoon when a car came up behind me. It pulled up beside me and stopped. Two young men, maybe in their twenties, were inside. They rolled down the window and called to me.

"Hi," they said, and asked me if they could give me a ride.

How nice of them! I thought, to see a young girl walking along and offer to help.

"Thank you," I said. "But, no. I'm fine." I continued to walk on.

They drove along beside me. "You sure you're okay? We're happy to give you a ride."

I again declined, and thanked them.

They continued to follow me for almost two blocks, attempting to engage me through the window, until finally they drove off.

After I'd gotten home, I got a call from my parents. Knowing that they'd been worried, I recounted the experience to them, hoping to convince them of the great choice I had made. See what a great neighborhood I lived in, where people were so solicitous?

It was later that evening when I had the visit from my stepmother. To me, her response seemed extreme, and I reacted to it as if it were a form of control. I nearly slammed the door in her face.

Looking back, it's something I now deeply regret, because she saw what I didn't see.

I dodged a bullet that night.

The reality, I now realize, is that I was a conspicuous target: a reasonably attractive young girl alone, at dusk, not particularly aware of her surroundings.

When it comes to being out on your own, understanding safety rules is crucial. I had a lucky escape. Many others haven't. What should I have done differently? And what other skills should someone learn in order to avoid getting into a scary situation?

That's what this chapter is all about.

The Basics

Most of the adults on the spectrum that I've spoken with have had similar experiences with safety concerns. These issues tend to cluster in certain key areas that we will cover in this section. As you start heading out into the world, here are a few considerations to focus on in order to keep yourself safe.

Stranger Danger

You may recognize the phrase "stranger danger" from grade school safety talks. It still applies in adulthood. Those on the spectrum tend to be more trusting than most, and our difficulties in reading the nonverbal cues of others can open us to additional danger. So, it's important that you take a few precautions when it comes to interacting with others.

It can be difficult for those of us on the spectrum to identify warning signs that suggest someone isn't trustworthy. When you are dealing with a stranger—or just getting to know someone—it's important to be cautious. In some situations, you may need to rely on someone else's judgment. Many routine activities are more socially demanding than one might expect.

For example, situations that involve buying, selling, or negotiating are particularly demanding from a social standpoint. In these cases, it can be important to have a trusted friend or relative who is more skilled at reading social cues come along with you to help guide you through the interaction. This person will be able to identify warning signs that you may not see.

In Our Own Words

Because we [people on the autism spectrum] cannot read others' intentions well, we need to be hyper alert to the possibility of harm or bullying of any kind. I depend on others to help me discern who is good and who might be risky or dangerous. This means I have to disclose [information] to some people [who] I may not want to just so they can help me. —Liane Holliday Willey, senior editor of the *Autism Spectrum Quarterly* and founder of the Asperger Society of Michigan

What if you're not in a position to rely on someone else? What if you don't have someone you feel you can trust? Or if another person isn't available, what are some strategies that you can use to identify whether someone might be a threat, without unduly limiting yourself?

Planning is one very important and useful strategy that you can use. A common trait of those of us on the spectrum is to prefer predictability. Many aspects of common tasks are predictable, if you plan ahead. When you approach situations that may expose you to unfamiliar people, such as common tasks like going to the store, or washing your clothes at the Laundromat, you can break down these tasks into key components and put those components together like a puzzle.

To help you form your strategy, ask yourself a few questions:

- What are you attempting to accomplish?

- Who will you need to interact with in the course of completing that task?

- What level of interaction will be required and when?

Imagine you're going grocery shopping, for example. What do you need to accomplish? What items do you need to purchase? In the process, who are some types of people you will need to interact with?

A cashier? Probably. A pharmacist? Maybe. Other shoppers? Perhaps, but on a more limited basis. A manager? Possibly, if you need additional assistance with an issue. But what about a person who is loitering in front of the store? What interaction is necessary?

Probably none.

If a person like this is persistent in his or her attempts to engage you, it's worthwhile to be careful. This is also true if a person approaches you seeking interaction beyond what might be needed for the task required. What if, for example, another shopper approaches you asking for money, or is trying to sell you something? They may be harmless, but they could also be up to no good. If they are, it may not always be immediately obvious.

If their intentions are unclear, this is a cause for concern, and it's important to be cautious. We are socialized to be kind and polite to everyone, but in some cases it may even be necessary to be rude. If it's a question of politeness or safety, sometimes it's important to err on the side of safety.

Self-Knowledge and Strategy

One of the key components of building a successful life is learning how to navigate through your particular mix of strengths and weaknesses. Knowledge is power. Ask yourself: What are you good at? In what areas do you need a little more assistance? What are some strategies for minimizing your challenges while maximizing your unique abilities?

Some people on the spectrum, for example, may have trouble with speech, or may lose the ability to speak unexpectedly under stress. So, it's important to plan ahead. If you are out and about, how will you communicate with others? Will you need assistive technology?

It's very important to know how you will communicate during very tense situations, such as a medical emergency, or an interaction with the police. One option is an autism disclosure and education card that can be handed out to first responders or medical professionals. This can help to minimize misunderstandings in stressful situations when articulation and communication may become more difficult. Generic preprinted cards are available from national organizations, such as the Autism Society (*www.autism-society.org*).

You can also make a custom card for yourself, tailored to your specific needs. Here are some typical items that you would want to include:

- Your diagnosis (or diagnoses) and a short description of what that means

- Common behaviors (especially those that may be misunderstood) such as not looking a person in the eye, self-stimulating behavior like rocking or hand flapping

- Differences in processing pain (hypo- or hypersensitivity to pain)

- Allergies, medications, or other medical needs

Another point that I, and many others on the spectrum, have had to learn the hard way is one that is relatively simple: *Learn when to ask for help.* This can be particularly difficult for those of us on the spectrum. But it's important to remember that *all* of us—whether on the spectrum or not—have situations where we must reach out to others. It's nothing to be ashamed of.

Take stock of your particular profile of skills. What are some areas where you might need some additional help?

- Fixing things around the house?

- Managing finances?

- Identifying "unsafe" people?

- Navigating challenging social interactions, such as negotiating for a car?

If so, it's okay to ask for help. This can be hard for many of us who've experienced rejection due to the help we've needed in the past. So, how do we avoid having our need for help drive this kind of rejection?

How do we avoid creating the impression that we are "using" another person? It's all about *reciprocity*, a key concept that's important for those of us on the spectrum to learn. People reject us when they perceive that we take more than we give.

This is why it's very important to know your strengths. You have something to give, too. Work to identify what those things are.

Ask yourself:

- What do you have to offer that may help others?

- How can you best leverage those strengths?

Once you've answered these questions, you can use this awareness to develop win/win relationships centered around specific skills: skills you have that they need; and skills *they* have that *you* need.

In Our Own Words

Don't rely too much on any one person. It will burn them out. Instead, create "strategic partnerships," based on specific skills and abilities. —Brian R. King

Boundaries

Another point heavily emphasized by adults on the spectrum is the subject of boundaries. What is a boundary? In the physical world, a boundary is a structure that protects what's inside from what's outside. The walls, doors, and windows of your house are boundaries that serve to protect your belongings inside from harm, which can come in many forms: rain, snow, wind, damage from other people, or from being stolen by thieves.

Interpersonal boundaries serve a similar purpose. Interpersonal boundaries are rules that you set about how others can engage with you, therefore protecting yourself from harm. Like physical boundaries, interpersonal boundaries protect from someone doing physical or emotional harm to you, whether it's by stealing things that are yours, by beating you, hurting your feelings, or by taking actions that negatively impact the quality of your life.

When you are a child, you are given limited autonomy to set these boundaries; however, as you grow older, into your teen and adult years, society begins to allow you more and more latitude to set boundaries. As an adult, you have a right to set boundaries with the people around you. They also have the right to set boundaries with you.

When you set boundaries, others should respect them. When others set boundaries, you should do your best to respect them as well. If there are times that your boundaries clash with another person's boundaries, then you will need to negotiate a compromise. For example, when in an argument, one person may become overwhelmed and need to set a boundary for herself by withdrawing from the confrontation. The other person's boundary is that leaving during a conversation, especially an important one, is rude and disrespectful. Talk about these two boundaries and the needs behind them. A solution might be that you make an agreement where the person withdraws for a specific period of time, then promises to come back and have the conversation. Thus, each person gets a little bit of what he or she wants.

Each person's right to set boundaries should be respected; however, it isn't fair to another person in the relationship if one person's boundaries negate the other's. In relationships (whether family, friend, or romantic partner), both people should get as many of their needs met as possible. A fair boundary should take this into account. Thus, boundaries that are too one-sided are not appropriate. For example, it's a fair boundary to say, "If we watch TV, I should be able to watch something I would like to watch some of the time." It is *not* an appropriate boundary to say, "If we watch TV together, we should always watch what I want to watch, and you should like it."

Setting boundaries can be difficult or uncomfortable for those of us on the spectrum for a number of reasons, one of which is social pressure. The unfortunate reality for many on the spectrum is that the training that we receive to help us to "blend in" to the wider world can have the difficult side effect of teaching us to ignore our own boundaries.

We learn to tolerate pain and discomfort of situations beyond what many others experience in order to appear more "normal" or to "fit in." While learning such skills can be useful in some situations, it's also important to learn to recognize when a situation is too painful or uncomfortable for us, or when it could lead us into actual harm.

In Our Own Words

It's not safe to have no boundaries. It's a way to get assaulted, harassed, and abused. So set some, and stick to them. —Alyssa Zisk, Adult on the Autism Spectrum

From the time I was a little girl, my mother had a saying that she emphasized very strongly. She would say, "No one has the right to touch you in any way that you aren't comfortable with. You *always* have the right to say 'No.' It's your body, not theirs." Remembering this advice has served me well. Sadly, there are a lot of people who will attempt to take advantage of social naiveté, or even use force, to try to coerce a young woman or man into doing something that she or he is not comfortable with.

Because it's more difficult for us to "read" unwritten social rules in order to determine appropriate physical boundaries, it may be necessary to be more explicit than those who are not on the spectrum. When in doubt, ask. Asking outright helps to minimize the chances of misreading a social situation, and accidentally violating someone else's boundaries.

In Our Own Words

What people say isn't always the truth, —Máire Shortt, Adult on the Autism Spectrum

Also, by clearly setting boundaries with others in this way, you set an example for those who interact with you. This makes it easier to request the same of others. If they later initiate contact that you are not comfortable with, and they have *not* asked permission to initiate that kind of contact, then you are perfectly within your rights to say, "No," or "I'm not comfortable with your touching me in that way."

Another aspect of setting boundaries involves identifying and protecting yourself from those who may seek to exploit you. In some situations, you can help to protect yourself by relying on a trusted person to vet new acquaintances. If that is not possible, then it's important to watch for certain suspicious behavior.

Suspicious behavior covers a lot of area (some of which we will cover more in depth later in the book), but some warning signs might be:

Excessive interest in your belongings or valuables. Do they ask about your money, or where you keep it? Do they ask to borrow valuable items like an iPad, car, or computer after a very short acquaintance?

Do they show actual interest in you as a person, or do they always contact you to make a request that you do something for them? Do you hear from them only when they need help of some kind?

How respectfully do they treat you? Do they tell you they are your friend while saying hurtful things about you behind your back or to your face?

If they ask you to do things, are they activities that will get you into trouble? Do they ask you to do something immoral, or illegal? If so, treat them very carefully. They most likely do not have your best interests in mind. If something feels wrong, it very often is!

In Our Own Words

We should all learn to trust our instincts. —Liane Holliday Willey

Boundaries and Family

At this point in your life, it will become very important to learn to adjust your boundaries in life, especially around family. As you grow into your teen and adult years, your needs for independence and support will change. This is natural. It is a part of human development—this is a drive the pushes you to begin developing the autonomy that you'll need later as an adult. For most people, this doesn't happen suddenly; it's a gradual process that begins for most people far before the day that they reach the age of eighteen. It can create a problem when parents don't recognize the reality of this need, or the purpose of this need.

If they are very close and protective of their child, it can be hard for them to cope with the fact that their child wants and needs time away from them. For other parents, the problem can be the opposite. They may recognize the need for their child to be independent and develop self-reliance, but feel that their child isn't taking enough initiative in this. These parents will push their kids very hard, sometimes too hard. This can cause stress and conflict.

In order to make it through this period of your life, you need to develop the skills to recognize if your family dynamics have become destructive for you. Do you find yourself feeling stifled, unable to grow, because of the limits placed on you? Do you find yourself getting depressed, because you feel incompetent? Is your stress so high, you sometimes wonder if you could really function, or you fear that you will lose control? These may be signs that the dynamics of your relationships with others are having a damaging effect on you.

Setting Boundaries with Family

So, what do you do when you recognize that dynamics like these are causing issues with family members? The first thing is to learn to communicate to your family members the negative impact their actions or words are having on you. This can be difficult, especially if things have progressed to the point that you have had a meltdown or have become depressed. Sometimes, it requires that you take some time for self-contemplation and exercising of some of the self-awareness techniques we discussed earlier in this book.

Once you've been able to identify exactly what you're feeling, then you need to plan what you will say. You also need to prepare yourself emotionally for the conversation. In these types of situations, the other person will usually resist what you have to say. You will need to have the calm and the confidence in order to state what you feel, and what you need, even though someone is fighting the validity of what you are saying. One of the key skills you'll need to learn as an adult is when and how to trust your own feelings and instincts about a situation, and to stand up for your feelings appropriately.

If you can, see if you can get your family members to set aside some time to talk. You will be at a disadvantage (and the talk probably won't go well) if you try to have the conversation when they're busy doing something else and not giving you their full attention. Before the talk, take a few moments to do things that calm you. Take deep breaths, listen to soothing music—anything that will calm you. Rehearse what you want to say, and try to anticipate how they might respond and how you will respond to those responses.

When you finally have the conversation, make sure you give the conversation your full attention. Be prepared for the possibility that your family members may not recognize the impact of their actions on you, and they may be confused, or they may not understand what you're saying. Try not to be frustrated. Remember the times that you've struggled to understand something and others were patient with you. Try to treat your family members the same way. If they don't get it, try to figure out what they do not understand, and try to break the problem down in such a way that they will get it.

Imagine that, while at college, you have a job at a local grocery store. The manager has cut the amount of hours you were scheduled to work; you feel this is unfair, and you're frustrated. You ask your mother about what to do, but instead of giving you advice on how to approach and resolve this problem yourself, she begins angrily venting about your jerk manager. Later on, she drives down to the store without telling you and has an angry confrontation with him.

You get to work for your next shift to find her in your manager's office, yelling. Finally she storms out. For the rest of the day, your coworkers tease you for having your "mommy" do the "dirty work" for you; your manager is rude to you all evening and angrily tells you that if you had a problem with his scheduling choices, you should have been "adult enough" to have dealt with him directly. You're embarrassed and try to apologize. You say she did this without your knowledge, but you're not sure he believes you. What do you do?

Before you do anything, try to take some time to sort out your feelings. Are you angry? That wouldn't be surprising. But what else are you feeling? Are you sad that your mother didn't think that you could handle this on your own? Are you embarrassed by how her actions made you appear to your coworkers? Are there any positive feelings you have about the situation, like gratitude? As flawed as the tactics she used are, they prove one thing: She was angry that someone did something to cause you discomfort or frustration, and took immediate action to try to change that. The most logical reason behind doing this is that she loves you. That's a good thing.

Once you've got a good sense of what you're feeling, then sit down alone and plan out what you will say to her. Try to sequence your remarks in a specific way. First, begin by expressing what was positive about the situation. If there wasn't anything you can think of, say something you appreciate in general about your mom. "Mom, I know that you really love me. You heard how frustrated I was about the way my hours were cut and tried to fix that. You were trying to help me, and I appreciate that."

This makes the next bit you will say easier for the person to hear. It lets the person know that you do see the good, whether it is something that's generally good about her, something she did right in the situation, or the good intentions you know that she had. The next part of what you need to say is to clearly state the problem, what you disliked about what she did, and why. "However, when I brought up this issue to you, I hoped that you would explain to me how to handle the situation myself. I want to be able to be independent, and in order to do that, I'll need to know how to do this myself."

Next, explain how her actions affected you, both socially and emotionally. "When I came into work today, and saw you arguing with Bob, I felt very embarrassed. It was as if you thought I didn't have the capacity to learn the skills I needed to handle the situation myself. That made me feel as if you didn't think I was smart, and that made me sad. When my coworkers heard about it, they assumed that I couldn't handle it either and began teasing me about needing my 'mommy' to solve my problems for me. In addition, Bob reprimanded me and said that in the future he expected me to be 'adult enough' to handle conflict directly with him."

Finally, finish where you began, by expressing the positive again, but follow up by stating clearly what you would prefer she do in the future, and why. "Again, mom, I really appreciate that you had my concerns at heart, but in the future I would really prefer it if you would help me to handle things myself, rather than just taking care of it. This way, I can effectively learn the skills I need to learn to be more independent, and that would help me to build confidence. Using those skills in front of the guys at work will show them that I'm not a mama's boy."

After you say this, she may apologize, and say, "Ok, that's what I'll do next time." Or she may express concerns that you will make mistakes if you handle stuff like that alone. If she does, acknowledge what she has said, but restate your request: "You're right, I might make a mistake. However, making mistakes is how we learn. If I don't have the opportunity to make mistakes on my own, I don't have the opportunity to learn. The way you could help me best is to be there to advise me if I do make those mistakes." As an adult, you have the right to have preferences about what people around you do or say that impact you negatively.

When Family Members Don't Respect Boundaries

There will be family members (and others) who don't respect your boundaries. You will reasonably communicate your boundary, and they will continue to willfully violate it. Depending on how sensitive the person is, and how much she cares about you, stopping this behavior may be as simple as continuing to restate and reinforce that boundary. Imagine you've had a conversation like we discussed earlier with your mother about allowing you to handle work situations yourself, yet she goes to talk to your manager again. If you value this boundary, then you want to make sure she understands how important it is to you.

You'd say something like, "I heard today from Bob that you went to talk to him. Mother, I know we discussed this before, but as much as I appreciate your looking after me, it's really important to me that I learn to do these things myself, and to get the respect from my coworkers that comes from their seeing me as an equal. What you are doing is standing in the way of that. Please don't do that again." In this scenario, you're restating what you want, but you are being a little more direct about it. This shows her that you are serious, that it's important, that you feel strongly about it.

Unfortunately, sometimes when you're setting a boundary over something like this, it may be a behavior that is ingrained. They may forget your request in the emotions of the moment. They may also think, "Oh, he was just having a bad day and was being cranky. I'll just do it this once and it will be okay." This is why you communicate that it is not. Then they realize that your request was not a one-time-only request, but is something you consider a requirement for dealing with you going forward.

Sometimes, you'll find that even when you continue to reinforce your boundaries, people will continue to violate them. If they are friends, then you might decide to no longer be friends with them. If they are family, it may be harder. In these cases, you need to continue setting boundaries, but you may need to apply some more stringent consequences than simply having them hear that you're upset. These consequences should be related to the severity of the violation (or cumulative amount of violations) to your boundaries.

Some people will put a lot of pressure on you when you begin to enforce boundaries, implying that they are unreasonable, or accusing you of being mean. If you've chosen your boundaries in a fair manner, considering others in the process, then it is unlikely that this is true. This is simply a tactic that they are using to get you to let them do what they want. If you feel your boundaries are fair, continue to enforce them.

Some friends or family members may get angry. They may yell at you. They may escalate their bad behavior in response to your boundary setting. These are acts designed to try to gain back the control they are losing over you (especially if they are used to not having boundaries set by you at all). Recognize this, and stand your ground. Eventually, they will realize that you're not going to back down, and they will adapt.

Sometimes, setting a boundary is not about stopping what others do, but stopping what you do for others. For example, if you have a family member with addiction issues, you might set a boundary that you will no longer get up at 2 A.M. to pick him up from a bar because he can't drive, when you have work at 6 A.M. the next day. As an adult, it is his responsibility, not yours, to look after his own safety. While you may worry about what will happen to him if you don't rescue him, you are not obligated to take actions that will cost you your health or your job performance.

Setting boundaries is something you do because you care about your own well-being, as well as the well-being of others. Set them because you care for yourself, and consider your feelings and preferences worthy of being respected. If you have family members who do not respect appropriate boundaries, there may be times when it's appropriate to set the ultimate consequence: severing the relationship. If you do so, try to follow good boundary-setting procedures.

If you practice what we've discussed in this chapter, your family member will have ample warning before you take that ultimate step. Even if this is the case, they will still likely struggle with the decision. Only you can decide if their behavior is damaging enough (to you, or to them, or to both) that you're better off not having them in your life. If you feel you've made the right decision, stand by it. Trust your judgment.

Staying Physically Safe

For those of us on the autism spectrum, staying physically safe can present additional challenges. Aspects of autism, such as sensory issues, literal thinking, and differences in body language, can make us especially vulnerable. Staying safe will require you to become aware of how these things might affect safety and to come up with some creative solutions to address them.

Sensory Issues

Sensory issues can be an extreme source of stress for us, as you have no doubt experienced. As you become more independent, you will likely find that the sensory issues that cause pain and discomfort in your life today may affect you in ways that you might not have expected. When you go out in public alone, there will be times when sensory overload will put you in danger.

When I was about nineteen years old, I had to walk a mile or two from my apartment to get to work, through some pretty difficult parts of town. But the part that was my undoing was that this branch of the post office was located in downtown in the business district. The noise and bustle of this could be stressful on the best days. One particular day, it crossed from stressful to dangerous. I had just had a very stressful conversation with someone I cared about before I left to go to work.

This exacerbated my sensory issues. So when a driver made a dangerous turn, without noticing that I was in the crosswalk, I did not see the car in time to get out of the way. The car hit me and sent me flying about ten feet. Fortunately, because of the crowds, the driver was not going very fast and I escaped some of the worst injuries that could have occurred. But the jolt permanently damaged my hearing. What I learned from that experience was that self-awareness was crucial for my safety.

Nowadays, before I leave the house, I will always take a few minutes to check my physical state and take a few deep breaths. You may find this useful to practice in your own life. If you are very overwhelmed, you might make the tough choice not to leave the house.

While it may be ideal to wait to go out until your body naturally calms itself, through isolation or other techniques, there will be times when it will not be an option. For example, when it comes to employment, punctuality will very likely be part of the job requirement. If so, you will need to figure out some alternate ways to deal with such conflicts, such as identifying some techniques that you can use to quickly calm yourself enough so that it is safe for you to go out.

If you are having a particularly bad day, you may need to change how you normally get to work. In the situation I described, punctuality was a requirement, so not leaving the house at a specific time was likely to cost me my job if done often enough. If I had it to do over today, I might have chosen to get a taxi or to ask another person for a ride, because this would have minimized my exposure to traffic danger while still getting me to work on a timely basis.

When it comes to navigating environments containing a lot of sensory input, it can help to bring a companion with you who knows about your sensory challenges. This way your friend can help monitor for signs of overload and can help you navigate through the environment. Another precaution you may want to take is to put together a Sensory Emergency Kit—which would include, depending on your particular sensitivities, things like the following:

- Earplugs, earbuds, and music player, or noise canceling headphones, for auditory sensitivities

- A brimmed hat and/or sunglasses for difficulties with bright lights

- Snacks or drinks that you like, in case you cannot find foods that do not clash with your sensory sensitivities

- Gum, candy, or mouthwash to eliminate unpleasant aftertaste from unfamiliar food

- Extra clothing, to help with temperature sensitivities and/or to replace a piece of clothing that is creating tactile discomfort

- Items you can use to keep yourself occupied in a line or when you have to wait, such as games or handicrafts of some kind

- Objects you can use to calm yourself and that may make stimming less obvious, such as a worry stone, a piece of ribbon to stroke, or a stress ball to squeeze

- If you have extreme sensitivities to smell, you may be able to obtain a filter to put over your nose and mouth to minimize smells like perfume or heavy food smells

Body Language

Body language can create unexpected challenges for those of us on the spectrum, in a number of ways. The most obvious, of course, is the challenge with reading the body language of others, especially threatening body language. However, serious issues can also occur through the misunderstanding of our own body language and the nonverbal language of those with a neurotypical makeup.

One issue called out by many on the spectrum is something that one adult I interviewed calls "behavioral homonyms." These are behaviors and gestures that people on the spectrum sometimes make or do that appear the same as some typical body language cues amongst those with a neurotypical makeup. However, for someone on the spectrum, they may mean something entirely different.

Ennien Ashbrook says of behavior homonyms: "They look the same as gestures that neurotypical people do, but [they] convey different meanings—they can cause so many misunderstandings, in both directions. Flailing hands about is a gesture that I, like many people with AS [Asperger's syndrome], use when I'm exasperated; however, many neurotypical people interpret my gesture as aggressive, [or] possibly [an indication of my] becoming violent, even though I wasn't even close to that point yet. By the same token, I have missed signs of aggression in [people with a] neurotypical [makeup], because their waving arms communicated frustration to me, not aggression, so I hadn't realized that their situation had escalated so far."

When thinking of behavioral homonyms, some of the most obvious would be eye contact. As discussed previously, amongst people with a neurotypical makeup, eye contact is used as an indicator to show that you are interested and are paying attention to whomever is speaking. For most people on the spectrum, it really doesn't mean that at all. Unfortunately, the average neurotypical person whom you might meet would probably judge you as rude or inattentive if you don't make eye contact.

As unpleasant as that type of judgment is, it may not impact your safety unless the person you're dealing with is an authority figure such as a law enforcement professional or judge. If you did not make eye contact with the police officer who is interrogating you, for example, that could have serious repercussions. Unless you have made the officer aware of your diagnosis, the officer would likely interpret this as disrespect and/or dishonesty. This is why having informational cards you can hand out in such a situation can be so important.

There are also other behavioral homonyms that can prove particularly dangerous in the wrong setting. For example, some types of stimming can be misunderstood in catastrophic ways. A few years ago a man on the spectrum was shot and killed by police as he was walking home. It was after midnight, in an area prone to gang violence. Officers mistook some of his stimming and gestures as indications that he was reaching for a gun.

One way to avoid such situations is to build some self-awareness of the types of tics or stims that you display that may be misconstrued by others. It may be helpful to get input on this from people who know you well, such as your family. Watch yourself, or have them watch you during a time when you may be stressed but are in a safe environment. If they tell you that certain types of behaviors you portray may be misunderstood, you'll need to make some plans ahead of time as to how you will handle those behaviors when they appear in a situation where they could be perceived as threatening.

Mindfulness techniques can really help to calm yourself in difficult situations, thus avoiding the use of nervous stims, but when it doesn't work, another alternative is to develop alternate stims that may appear less threatening. For example, I rub a worry stone (a small stone with an indentation for my thumb) as an alternate to a stim that might be perceived as aggressive or disruptive to people who are not on the spectrum.

The benefit of an alternate stim is that it is less obvious than some others, like flapping. You can use it at times when you need to calm yourself but when a more obvious stim might prove problematic. You may have to try a few alternates to figure out what works best for you.

Behavioral homonyms can be particularly dangerous for females on the spectrum. One common worry for women is our vulnerability in terms of sexual violence. Unfortunately, a number of typical behavioral patterns in many women can be misconstrued by neurotypical males as signs of sexual interest. This may open you to sexual assault or harassment.

For example, some stims, such as playing with your hair or swinging your leg while you're sitting cross-legged in a chair, could be mistaken as flirting. The same may be true if you don't get eye contact just right—if you give too much eye contact, or you look at someone only briefly and turn away. For women, it may be wise to keep a trusted neurotypical friend nearby when you first meet a person of the opposite sex. That person can give you guidance or intervene if she recognizes that you are unintentionally sending the wrong signals to the person.

Also, it's a smart idea to read some of the pop culture articles written for men that discuss how to tell when a girl is "into you." As you read, think about how you typically interact in an encounter with a person of the opposite sex. If there are behaviors listed that are similar to behaviors that are common for you, but that have a completely different meaning, make adjustments for that in order to protect yourself.

There are times when you will *not* want to make eye contact. For example, for men, making eye contact while in the bathroom or at the urinal may be completely misunderstood. It may be perceived as a sign of interest in a sexual encounter, which can have some really uncomfortable consequences, if not wanted. Some particularly homophobic men may even become violent or hostile toward you if they feel that you are showing sexual interest in them.

Another place where eye contact may not be advisable is when you are in an enclosed space such as an elevator, crowded subway car, or bus. It is related to the concept of "personal space." A person's "personal space" is an area around his or her body that you are not meant to cross. This is an unspoken social barrier, which most people unconsciously expect you to respect—and it may vary based on the culture that person is from and the nature of your relationship to that person. In North America, you'll want to keep it least an arm's length away, if not more, from an average acquaintance.

When someone violates the boundaries of that personal space, it is usually experienced by the other person as a threat. This unconscious drive to keep people at a specific distance works alongside other indicators, such as eye contact. A person who violates another's personal space, while at the same time making prolonged eye contact, will be perceived as extremely aggressive and threatening. When you're out in the open, a person who is feeling threatened by this type of body language will either back away or become aggressive.

Enclosed places, such as elevators and public transit, may provide specific challenges with regard to this because you're often forced to violate a person's personal space. Because the person doesn't have the option of backing away, his options are limited, making hostility or aggression more likely. If you make too much eye contact while you're violating someone's personal space, it will worsen that discomfort and you may be perceived as creepy or potentially threatening.

Other instances where you'll need to be careful about extended eye contact are situations where you're in a crowded city, or perhaps at an airport—any place where there are a lot of people bustling back and forth, where crime is not atypical. These are places where people are especially on guard because the larger crowds increase the likelihood that there may be dangerous people around, so larger than typical personal space will likely be expected, but the fact that there are so many people may make it difficult to respect that personal space in every instance.

Because of this, it's important to avoid making prolonged eye contact with anyone, especially with those you don't know. In both the subway situation and the city street situation, acknowledge other people with a nod of the head and *brief* eye contact (if possible). Try practicing this in a mirror. Look your reflection in the eye (if you can), and count to three. This is what counts as a "brief" period of eye contact.

Unfortunately, as psychological research has proven, dangerous people are often particularly good at picking out of a crowd those who are vulnerable. One of the common signs that they use to determine this vulnerability is body language. Some typical signs of body language patterns that they might zero in on are present in many on the autism spectrum. For example, some studies have shown that criminals are more likely target someone with a less fluent gait, or someone who fidgets a great deal.

To stay safe, you need to stay aware of your environment. When walking somewhere in an urban environment or with a lot of people, it's important to walk purposefully. Keep an end goal in mind, and if that destination or goal is not immediately visible, sometimes it can help to visualize it in your mind. But also remember, it's important not to get too caught up in your imagination but to stay in the moment so you are aware of your surroundings. Constantly scan any group or crowded area to make sure that there are no signs of someone making a sudden movement toward you or potentially lingering too closely.

When you think about what it means to appear dominant or submissive when it comes to body language, think about the concepts of large and small. If you look across the animal kingdom, dominant animals make themselves big—think about a gorilla charging, or even how dogs or cats bristle up and arch their backs when threatened. What does this mean for humans? They stand upright, with shoulders square. They stand with their feet further apart. Gestures will be bigger.

When it comes to submissive body language, it's about making yourself small. You might hunch and look down. Your gestures would be smaller. If you're standing, you might cross your legs at the ankles, thus appearing to take up less space. When you're in an area where safety is important, check your posture periodically. Are you making yourself smaller or larger? This can often mean the difference between appearing vulnerable or appearing strong.

Handling Money Safely

As you become more independent, there will be a lot of opportunities where you'll need to handle money. For physical safety, there are some rules that will help to make sure that you don't find yourself targeted by criminals, or find yourself in the position of losing your money. Some of these rules are more about logistics.

For example, if you are going shopping, and you have issues with manual dexterity, it can take a while to sort out the appropriate change for a given transaction. You may feel uncomfortable or intimidated when people get impatient with the delay in counting out change and/or when you are putting money away. Despite that feeling, it's a good idea to make sure you never leave the checkout without putting your money away. Guarding the security of your money is more important than inconveniencing others.

Rather than sacrificing your security, find a way to manage the impatience of those around you. Often, you can get people to give you a little more leeway if you simply acknowledge their presence and that you know that they are waiting. If you notice you're taking a little bit longer than some of the other people around you, or you see people behind you tapping their foot or looking around at other lines to see if there's a quicker line that they could switch to, you might look at them and say something like, "Sorry, I'll be out of your way in a minute." Or you might say, "If you could just bear with me a moment, I'll gather up my stuff and be out of your way." Statements like this one may defuse possible conflicts. It may not dissuade some of the less tolerant people you'll encounter, but I've often found it to help.

You should also be prudent in how you handle your wallet or billfold. If you are a man, and you carry your wallet in your pocket, always make sure to put it in your pocket before you leave the store. You don't want to accidentally leave it behind. You may also want to consider keeping your money directly in your pocket. If you do that, you don't have to take out your whole wallet and risk dropping it.

For women, if you carry a purse, you'll want to put your wallet or billfold in the purse and fasten it securely before you leave the store. It's also a good idea to carry your purse in such a way so that pickpockets don't have easy access. If you carry a backpack, you'll want to make sure that anything valuable is placed in a zippered pocket and fastened securely. You may want to consider reserving an inner pocket for valuables rather than an outer pocket, as an outer pocket will be easier for someone to sneak into while the backpack is on your back.

Whatever the format of the bag or purse you're carrying, fasten it securely and do what you can to cover the opening or fastening so that no one but you can easily reach or open it.

Pay special attention to your purse or wallet if there is a disruption in front of you. Some predators will work in teams. One will distract shoppers so that the other can reach in or snatch a purse or wallet while the owner's attention is elsewhere.

For bags with longer straps, which may be easy to slide off of your shoulder or easily cut, you'll want to take extra precautions. To prevent it from sliding off your shoulder, you may be able to put the strap over your head to the opposite shoulder, which will also often bring the bag itself close under your arm, so that you can hold onto the bag part itself and not just the strap. This way if someone tries to cut it or if the strap breaks, you'll have a secondary grip and will notice right away. Predators look for a purse or wallet that is easy to grab—so make it as hard as you can for them to do so!

If your bank issues you a debit card/bank card, it's important to safeguard the personal identification number (PIN) that is assigned. Make sure you memorize it right away. If you have trouble remembering it, don't write it down and keep it in your wallet. Banks are insured, and they will usually reimburse you money that is stolen from your account if your debit card is stolen. However, most often they will *not* reimburse you if they find out that your PIN was in your wallet along with the card. Your PIN is the equivalent of the password on your computer. It's what tells the automated system that you are you. Don't make it easy for anyone else to pose as you.

Because of the stress of dealing with people, you may be tempted to use the automated teller at the bank more often than do other people. If you do, there are a few rules that are good to follow when doing so to keep yourself and your money safe. If the machine looks as if it's been tampered with in any way, don't use it. Some criminals will tamper with automatic teller machines (ATMs) in order to get your PIN and debit card number so that they can steal your money.

Be careful about using ATMs that are in isolated areas, and avoid using poorly lit walk-up ATMs after dark. If you use a drive-up ATM, take notice of who is around you. A criminal may follow you into the enclosure to attack you and/or steal your card and PIN. If a car pulls up behind you, make note. Also look for pedestrians standing around when you drive up. People may reach in and grab your money or grab your ATM card. If a car is at the ATM in front of you, make sure it exits before you make the transaction. That car in front could block you in while someone else grabs your money or ATM card.

When you are using your debit card at a store or to obtain money from an ATM, pay attention to who is around you. Any time you use your debit card with the PIN, place your body and arms in front of the keypad in order to block anyone from seeing the numbers you enter. Be careful if any person stands too close to you in these situations as well. They should not stand right behind you, where they would be able to read over your shoulder. Common courtesy dictates that people waiting to use a walk-up ATM stand back a reasonable distance while you conduct your transaction. Don't feel self-conscious about asking others to give you "personal space" to conduct your transaction—it's about your safety.

Try to develop the habit of immediately putting your debit/credit card back into your wallet after using it. You'll also want to count your money to make sure that you received the correct amount. But when you do so, make sure you do so in an area where you're not seen by a lot of people. Look through the bills by looking at the top corner only while shielding the rest. This is especially true if you have just taken out a large sum of money. You don't want someone who is unscrupulous to see that you carry a large amount of cash.

If you go to the ATM during daylight hours when the bank is open, it will be easier to raise the issue if you do not receive the right amount of money. You would then be able to walk into the bank and report the issue to a teller or manager. If you go in the evening, you may need to call their customer service line, or come back during their business hours. Be sure to keep the receipt from the transaction until the issue is resolved. The sooner you are able to report the issue, the better off you are, so whenever possible, it would be a good idea to use the ATM during business hours.

If you keep your money in your pocket, put the smaller bills on the outside and the larger ones on the inside. This makes the more commonly used bills easier to access and shields the total dollar amount from onlookers. If you use a wallet, you might split the money into smaller groups. You might take a bill and put it in the main compartment of your wallet, but put the rest in a less visible pocket or compartment and take new bills out only as needed, putting them in the main compartment. This way, if other shoppers happened to catch a glimpse into your wallet when you open it to get your money out to pay, they will only see a small portion of what you actually have. This way, they may be less tempted to steal your wallet.

When getting money from an ATM or conducting any kind of credit card or debit card transaction on an automated machine (for example, when getting gas), it's crucial to guard your personal information. While the systems are designed for security purposes not to display your entire debit or credit card number, it's still best not to leave that kind of information lying around. After your transaction, make sure that you remember to retrieve your receipt. Nowadays, you will often be asked if you even want one.

Having a receipt is important for balancing your checkbook later on, or to use as proof if your card is charged incorrectly, so you'll want to get one. If you request a receipt, and at the end of the transaction the receipt doesn't come out, talk to a clerk or a teller to notify him that this occurred. This may be because the machine is out of paper and it may print the receipt out after it's reloaded. If it does, you may not have control over what happens to the receipt (with your information on it).

Encounters with Law Enforcement

In the previous sections, we touched on some of the issues and problems that can arise when dealing with law enforcement. However, this chapter would be incomplete without going through this topic more specifically. Statistics show that those of us who have differences often have a higher chance of coming into contact with those in law enforcement—sometimes because our differences are mistaken as being dangerous, because we need help, or because we find ourselves the target of a crime.

If you are stopped by a police officer, always be respectful and polite. This means saying "Yes, sir" or "No, ma'am." If asked for identification or for your license or registration, if you're in a car, provide it immediately. If it is dark when you are stopped, remember police officers are on guard and apprehensive about what they will encounter. Help them to see that you are not a threat by staying buckled in your seat, turning on the interior light in the car so the officer can easily see you and the inside of your car, and keep your hands visible on the wheel. If you are concerned as to how your body language or speech patterns may be perceived by the officer or first responder, let her know that you have autism and/or provide an autism information card. Before you reach for the card, however, indicate to the officer either verbally or with gestures that you will be reaching into your pocket or wherever the card is located so that the officer will not think you are reaching for a weapon.

No matter how unfair a situation may appear to you, do not argue with the officer. If he asks you to step out of a car or wait in a particular area, in a particular position, do so. Comply with any orders he gives you. No matter how stressed you may feel in the moment, do your best to remain calm. Perhaps take a few breaths. Do not make any sudden movements. If you are being accused of a crime, either verbally or through the use of an information card, state that you invoke the right to remain silent and ask to be represented by an attorney. If you are the victim of a crime, and you feel you need assistance, ask the officer to contact someone you trust who can advocate on your behalf, such as a friend or family member.

In Our Own Words

One great tip for law enforcement dealings I've found—do not show your frustration. Nothing gets you in trouble faster. —Susie R., Adult on the Autism Spectrum, editor in chief and head blogger at *www.insatiablebooksluts.com*, winner of the IBBA for Adult Fiction

If you hear, "Don't move! Police," this means you need to stop immediately, face the officer, and put your hands up in the air, with your palms toward the officer, so that he can see that you are not holding a weapon. If they say this to you, it is an indication that they believe that you may be dangerous or criminal, and that they are likely to arrest you. You need to do what they say. If you try to run away, or walk toward them, or do anything except stay still, these behaviors may confirm their suspicions about how dangerous you might be. If so, they may act to protect themselves, by shooting you or shocking you with a Taser gun.

Although it's not common, there have been incidents where people have impersonated police officers in order to attack or rob people. If a police car turns on its lights behind you when you are in a particularly isolated area, you can choose to wait to stop until you are in a populated area—just don't speed away. Keep driving slowly with the police behind until you find an area you feel comfortable to stop in. Go slowly enough to make it clear to the officer that you see them there and that you are not going to run away. If you want additional confirmation, you may want to consider calling the police department to confirm that there is an officer patrolling that particular area. If they indicate that there is not a policeman in the area, tell them that there is someone impersonating an officer and ask for direction as to what to do. They may want to send an officer out to apprehend the person.

Final Note

Safety is a big topic. I have tried to cover some of the most common and important considerations in this chapter; however, it is impossible to cover every eventuality that you may encounter. One of the best things that you can do for yourself is to become aware of the safety resources available to you in your area. Contact disability and autism-related organizations in your area to ask them if they have specific guidelines or resource lists available that are tailored specifically to the needs of adults with autism.

Consider taking self-defense courses (if they overwhelm you from a sensory standpoint, you may want to watch for a while first). You can also attend lectures put on by the local police and fire department. Many local libraries and/or employers host seminars on safety-related topics, such as preventing identity theft or fire safety. If you have specific challenges with regard to particular medical conditions (such as dealing with seizures or loss of consciousness due to low blood sugar), many service organizations, hospitals, or health plans put on free or low-cost classes regarding this. Check message boards at your local library, or do a search on Google.

Also, it may be very helpful to join a support group in your area. Being able to interact with and share tips and solutions with others like you can be very powerful. Local organizations can probably give you some ideas, or you can look to some national organizations like GRASP (*http://grasp.org*) that maintain lists of support groups, professionals, and resources on a state by state basis.

POINTS TO REMEMBER

- Learn when to ask for help. Find a few people who can help to support and advise you.

- Plan ahead. Identify the activities you may need to engage in to accomplish your goal. Be aware of interactions that fall outside those predictions.

- Consider keeping an autism disclosure and education card, if you feel you may have trouble communicating in stressful circumstances. Examples and samples of such cards can be found at *www.autism-society.org*.

- Establish your personal boundaries, and make it clear to others when they infringe on those boundaries. Be wary of people who do not respect those established boundaries.

- Sensory overload can put you in danger, so you will need to become aware of the warning signs.

- If you are overloaded, sometimes it's best to stay where you are until you calm down, even if it makes you late.

- If you are going into potentially overloading situations, have a sensory safety kit to deal with the potentially overloading stimuli.

- Body language differences can cause others to misunderstand us in ways that can be dangerous. Especially beware of "behavioral homonyms."

- When you're out and about, handle money carefully to avoid being targeted by robbers. Avoid using ATMs after dark.

- Always treat police officers respectfully and comply with their commands.

CHAPTER 5

Moving Away from Your Family

When you hear the word "independent," as it applies to you, what do you think? Do you think about being in your own place and making your own decisions? Many do. What does it take to have your own place? Do you want one, for now? What kind of work will it take to maintain your home? In this chapter we'll talk about just these things. What will you need to do to plan for living away from home? What are the pros and cons of living with a roommate? How do you choose a place that is safe to live?

We'll talk about things like leases and bills. We'll discuss how to build a budget, and how to choose what will be in it. We'll cover how to choose a roommate, if you choose to have one, and what things you should absolutely avoid. We'll talk about some of the tools and techniques that may help you to manage household chores, and how to get help with the things you struggle with. Finally, we'll talk about organization and time management, the skills you'll need in order to bring all these things together.

Choosing the Right Living Arrangement

Adulthood is an exciting time in your life, because you have the opportunity to start making some decisions of your own. One of those decisions will be where and how you want to live. There are a lot of considerations to this, some of which are personal and some of which are financial. It's a decision that will need a lot of planning.

You'll do the least amount of planning if you choose to remain living with your parents for a period of time. This may allow you a more gradual transition to living fully independently. However, you may chafe at the restrictions placed on your life by your parents. How limiting this may be depends on your parents and how they run their household. Some may be very strict, expecting you to follow all the same rules that you followed through your school years, while others may be more relaxed.

You may find that they will renegotiate the terms of your living situation based on your new status as an adult. They may ask you to start paying rent or contribute to the expenses of maintaining the household. If you are capable of doing so, this is not an unfair situation. It also can be helpful because this provides you with an opportunity to start building the skills necessary for living independently, while still in a safe environment. It may be a good interim step, if you can deal with the limitations.

Another option is to find a roommate. A roommate can share expenses and household chores. However, it may be difficult if you are a person who needs a lot of alone time or who requires control of your environment. When you're considering this option, you'll need to think about the benefit it will give you in terms of controlling your living costs versus the potential challenges of sharing your living environment with another person (or other people).

You can also choose to rent your own apartment or living space. This is more expensive, but it allows you more control of your environment. You will still have neighbors, and you will still need to interact with the owner or management of the apartment or property, but you will have considerable alone time if you need it. A fourth, more long-term option, is to buy a house or condo. This requires enough money to make a down payment and the necessary credit to obtain a mortgage on the property. Most people will choose to rent for a bit while saving the necessary money to be able to buy a house.

If you are leaving high school and going into college, many universities have dorms that are available for students. These are usually on campus, and are more reasonable than off-campus housing. However, many schools will require you to have a roommate. If you do not feel that this will work for you due to sensory and related issues and stress, you may be able to request a private room or pay extra for one. If you work through the school's disability services group, they may be able to get you an exception based on the fact that you are a person with autism.

Another option for some, depending on your situation, need for support, and the money that you have available or are able to make, is subsidized housing provided specifically for people with disabilities. The type and availability of this housing varies based on your area of the country as do the requirements for eligibility. Utilizing this option will usually require considerable documentation of your diagnosis and how it impacts your ability to make enough money to obtain housing in other ways. Some of these homes will be shared with other adults, and there will be support personnel provided to help with daily needs or potential medical issues. To find out what's available in your area, you can contact any of your local disability or autism service organizations.

Planning and Preparation

The first step in the planning process will be to choose what it is you want to do. What is your preferred living arrangement? Are you leaving school, going away to college, or are you choosing to stay in the neighborhood where you grew up? The answer to these questions will help guide you as you assess your options. In the end, you may end up with an interim plan and a long-term plan. So it's important not to limit yourself in this thinking process by what you think is possible *in the moment*. You may not have the resources at this point to own your own home, but if that is your ultimate goal, that will be a consideration in your short-term plan.

If your long-term plan is to buy a home and you plan to get a mortgage, then you may want to make sure that you rent in your own name in order to develop a credit history. This may change how you approach any kind of shared living arrangement—depending on how you set up the relationship, your name may not be on the lease. If your name is not on the lease, this will likely affect whether your payment history shows up on your credit report.

In Our Own Words

Everyone has different motivations and different steps they can take to live their life. —Jason Ross, Adult on the Autism Spectrum

The second step in the planning process will be to identify what your costs will be and put them together into a budget. This may be challenging, because you may not know exactly what your costs will be until you choose where to live. So you will probably need to estimate a few of the items on your list. Begin first by considering the types of things that will need to be in your budget:

- Monthly rent

- Security deposit

- Utilities (natural gas, electric, water, garbage, cable TV, phone, Internet)

- Insurance (renter's insurance, health insurance)

- Transportation (car, gas, insurance, maintenance, taxi, bus pass)

- Furniture

- Food

- Cost of hobbies, interests

- Contingency/miscellaneous (a certain amount of money set aside for unexpected costs, such as a car repair)

If you currently have a job, then you can begin by estimating rent at about 30–40 percent of your salary. If you are not currently working, then you may need to look at different areas that you might live, think about the type of job you are interested in doing or can do, and see what those jobs typically pay in those areas. (When you are thinking about areas you might want to live, ask the opinion of someone you trust whether that is a safe area to live. When you go looking at apartments, you might want to take that person with you to get a second opinion.) There are many locations online you can use to estimate rental costs.

You can browse job advertisements in the area and look at the types of salaries advertised for the jobs you're thinking about, or you can also go to sites like *www.salary.com* and *www.payscale.com*, which will show you various ranges for specific jobs. In addition, you can check the website of the Bureau of Labor Statistics (*www.bls.gov*), a division of the government that publishes average hourly rates for specific jobs nationally, regionally, and in specific metropolitan areas. When doing this, recognize that these sites will only tell you general averages; it does not necessarily mean that you will make this amount of money. You can make more or you can make less.

Once you have a general idea of what kind of job you might be able to get and what you might be paid for it, then you can calculate a very rough estimate for rent based on it. The range of 30–40 percent of one's salary is what many people use as a general benchmark to prevent from paying rent that's too high. Once you have that in mind, you'll want to look at the paper and/or online listings for living arrangements to see what the costs are in the areas where you might want to live. If the costs are above that 30–40 percent range, then you know that a particular area is out of your budget, and you may need to look elsewhere. If the cost is high for a single apartment, you may consider adjusting your expectations to allow for a roommate-type arrangement even if that wasn't what you had originally considered.

If the typical rents in the area where you want to live fall within the 30–40 percent range, then this gives you a place to start. You can then do some research as to the various options available in that area for utilities, including television, phone, and Internet.

You'll need to think about your patterns. How often do you like to eat out? How often do you buy supplies for a hobby or activity? Do you have any special dietary needs that make your food costs higher? Will you be able to drive, or will you take public transportation? Will you want renter's insurance in case someone breaks into your apartment and steals your belongings? Do you have a car? If you do, do you have a car payment? How about car insurance and money for gas and maintenance, such as oil changes and new tires?

Some of the costs in your budget will be one-time costs, such as a security deposit for an apartment, deposits to get utilities turned on, and purchases of large items like furniture or a car. Others will be ongoing, like your utilities and rent. If you add up all of the one-time charges, and one month's worth of the ongoing charges, you will know how much money you will need in order to get everything in place. If you don't have that amount of money, you'll have to figure out how to get it. You may need to consider getting the job in the area that you want to live while you still live in your current situation. Then, once you've saved enough money, you can move. In most cases, you will need to have a job or source of income to get a lease for an apartment.

One way around this is to have someone who has a job and regular income sign with you on the lease. What this means is that the person who signs on the lease with you guarantees that she will pay the rent if you don't. If she is willing to do this, it may be very helpful to you; however, if for some reason you do make a mistake and fail to pay your rent, it could negatively impact your relationship with that person. In addition, it means that this person may have a little more control over your life than you are comfortable with.

Overall, your budget should never exceed what you make in any given time frame. If you can plan your budget to stay at or below 90 percent of what you will make, you will be in a very good place. Because you are budgeting based on estimates, one particular line in your budget you want to pay specific attention to is the line for contingency/miscellaneous spending. You'll want to set this at about 10 percent of your overall budget. This is the amount you will set aside in a given month for any unexpected expenses, whether it be a blown tire on your car, an unexpected trip to the doctor, or any number of other costs that can come up in a month.

If you are unsure about your estimates, ask someone in your family or someone who is already out on her own to look at your proposed budget to make sure that you haven't forgotten anything and that it makes sense. There are also many resources (both online and off) to learn about budgeting and financial management. These are important topics to learn about, because these will impact whether you have the money to do the things you want to do in the future.

Living with Roommates

Depending on your personal situation, there may be times when living with a roommate is the preferable choice. You'll save money on rent and utilities, and split the tasks of household upkeep. But it also requires a lot of social interaction. When you live with someone, you will need to work through conflicts. For example, what if she likes to listen to loud music but you like it quiet? If you have very sensitive ears, would you be kept awake if your roommate decided to bring a date home and have sex? What if she likes to have a lot of people over? Would you feel uncomfortable?

Even if you know someone well, he may interact with you differently when living with you than he would in the other situations. Rules and expectations, such as routines, the frequency of chores, and how much certain things can be shared, vary widely from family to family. You will need to work out any differences in these attitudes with your roommate. In addition, if the person does not know about the difficulties you might have with nonverbal communication, it may cause you difficulties. He may expect that you just get it when he wants to be alone in the apartment, or he may be frustrated by some of your idiosyncrasies. You will have to decide whether to disclose your diagnosis, and how.

You may be able to prevent some difficulties by choosing your roommate carefully. If you are not moving in with a friend whom you know well, then you will probably want to have an extended conversation with your prospective roommate to see how well her interests, likes, and patterns work with yours. This is especially important in cases where you are considering a roommate arrangement with someone whom you just met.

In the first section of this book we talked about knowing yourself. You will need to use what you learned there. What do you like? What do you dislike? Which qualities do you think you could live with in a roommate, and which do you think you couldn't live with? You may want to make a list. Think about things like the following:

- Sound preferences (Do they like to listen to loud music?)

- Personality traits (Are they impatient or intolerant? Or understanding?)

- Are they steadily employed? (Will they be able to pay their appropriate share of the expenses in a timely manner?)

You might want to ask potential roommates about their family, and ask some salient facts about themselves. What do they do for a living? What do they like to do for fun? Do they like to go out, or do they like to stay home? What schedule do they work? Will they be up watching TV and hanging out with friends when you need to be sleeping? If they are evasive about your questions, especially those about employment, be cautious.

When considering a roommate, also consider whether you might be romantically attracted to a prospective roommate, or whether he might be romantically attracted to you. This could be difficult if only one of you develops feelings for the other that are not reciprocated, or if you try to explore a sexual relationship and things get out of hand. This could also be a problem if you move in with a romantic partner and later break up. How would you feel if you had six months left on your lease, and he is moving on to date other people, perhaps even bringing them home or having sex with them?

Once you've moved in with your roommate, if he makes any overtures toward you that are sexual and unwanted and does not stop when you ask him to stop, plan to get out as soon as possible. If a roommate crosses the line in terms of date rape or violence, don't tolerate it. Leave. This is a crime and it should be immediately reported. If you need to go back for your things, do not go alone. Get someone to go with you to protect you and make sure that the behavior doesn't happen again. If you don't have a friend or relative who is able to do this, then you may need to request police escort. If the person continues to harass you, then go to the police department and file a restraining order.

In a similar vein, if your roommate conducts any kind of illegal activities in your apartment, whether it's consuming illegal drugs or selling stolen merchandise, find a way out of that situation as soon as possible. If you ignore the crime going on in the apartment, you may be in trouble with the law even if you had nothing to do with the illegal activity. If your roommate is dishonest, he or she may pin the blame on you. Additionally, in some situations, if you are aware of a crime and do not report it, you will be considered an accomplice.

Another consideration when it comes to roommates is the structure of your arrangement. You'll have the most control if, when you get the apartment, you sign the lease and rent out the room. Before doing so, check with your landlord with regard to whether subletting is allowed according to your rental contract, and inquire with the city about local laws regarding subletting. The downside to this arrangement is that, with your name on the lease, you are liable for the entire rent and any cost if the apartment is damaged. You will also have to be the person to ask your roommate to leave if it doesn't work out. If your roommate does not pay, you will still be required to pay. To protect yourself, have a written agreement in place with a roommate laying out the rules and the amount and schedule of payment.

If your roommate has the lease on the apartment, you'll want to check to make sure that he is free to sublet to you, and have a written agreement documenting that you are subletting. Without an agreement, he could take your money and claim that it was a gift or payment for something else and not use it to pay for the rent. If he does not pay for long enough, you may be thrown out of your apartment, and you will have no way to sue the roommate for the money, because you will have no proof. If you have a written agreement showing that you are subletting, you were allowed to do so by law, and you have proof that the payment was made (a receipt or canceled check), you can sue to get your money back.

A final option is to look for the apartment together, and both sign the lease. In this situation the landlord knows that you are living there, and you are renting directly from him or her. How the payments are made will depend to some degree on how the lease was written; however, with both names on the lease, if your roommate does not pay his or her share and/or does damage to the apartment, you will also be liable for it, and they will also be liable if you don't pay or if you do damage to the apartment.

Roommate Etiquette

Whenever you live with someone you'll need to have a discussion about roles, responsibilities, and expectations. Once you've set those expectations, make sure you follow them. If you agree to take out the garbage every other week, then make sure that you do so. If there is some reason that you can't, talk to your roommate about making other arrangements.

Talk about schedules. Does she work the night shift or the day shift? Does it change sometimes? If so, talk about what that means in terms of her expectations of you. After what time does she prefer that you stay quiet and vice versa. Once you've discussed it and come to an agreement, honor it.

Will you each buy your own food, or will you share some or all of the food in the refrigerator? Who will do the food shopping? If you have special dietary needs, do you expect him to not eat your special food, or vice versa? Communication is very important. It doesn't hurt to capture it all in writing. A schedule posted on the refrigerator also clarifies things.

You'll also have to consider each other's schedule and patterns and how they impact one another. If you have one washer and dryer, how will it impact your roommate if you do your laundry but don't take it out of the dryer for a week? You may assume that your roommate will tell you if it's a problem and that she needs to use it, but she may feel she shouldn't have to. Then she would just get angry. Also, there are often times when a roommate might have an urgent need to use shared resources, such as the washer and dryer, when she might not be able to give you advance notice. If she is unable to use them because your laundry is only half done, that will be particularly frustrating.

Here are a few basic rules that will help:

- If you make food for yourself, clean up the crumbs and the dishes or put them in the dishwasher.

- Don't take or eat something that's not yours.

- If you eat the last of a particular food that you share, depending on your arrangement regarding shopping responsibilities, either buy a replacement or add it to a shopping list, so that your roommate will know it needs to be replaced.

- If you take something out, return it to the same place you found it so that it can be easily located.

- If you have memory or attention issues, set a timer or a reminder on your smartphone to prompt you to complete a task that you can't complete immediately.

- If something frustrates you or makes you mad, don't stew about it; discuss it.

Time Management and Prioritization

When you choose to live independently there are a number of responsibilities that come with it—things like housework, paying bills, and general maintenance of your environment. To live independently you will need to manage these responsibilities in an effective manner. Part of effectively managing your responsibilities is learning how to prioritize them. Sometimes thinking about all of the daily tasks you need to complete in order to keep your life in working order can be overwhelming, especially for someone who sees details first. What has helped me is to think about these tasks in specific groups. When you are overwhelmed, it can be tempting to do things that you enjoy or find easy first. Unfortunately this isn't always the best way to manage time.

In the corporate world, there is a time management technique, popularized by Stephen Covey in his books *First Things First* and *The 7 Habits of Highly Effective People*, which can be useful for prioritizing your responsibilities. First, you create a two by two matrix, with one axis being importance and the other being urgency. Then you look at each of the tasks on your list and assess where they would fit in that matrix. The result would look something like the table below.

	Urgent	Not Urgent
Important	Bills	Make out a will
Not Important	Buying a lottery ticket	Buying a cute pair of shoes

This is one way to visually represent how to prioritize what you need to spend the majority of your time on. When you look at the matrix, you want to spend the most time on the things that are both urgent and important, so they would be the highest priority on your to-do list. Since the things in the top right quadrant are important, then you'll want to prioritize them just after the stuff in the top left quadrant. The things in the bottom two quadrants are things that should be last in your priority list. If you are disciplined about looking at your tasks this way, it can really help to keep you on track.

Another way I find helps me to look at the tasks of daily living is by putting them in groups according to their consequences. For example, the consequences of not paying your bills are that you damage or ruin your credit, you may get your phone or electricity cut off, and you will have to pay more because of late fees. So these tasks are high-consequence tasks.

When dealing with high-consequence, very important, or very urgent items, such as paying bills, you need to handle them on a timely basis. Some bills can be paid online or can even be set up to automatically deduct from your bank account at the same time each month. If you find it difficult to keep up with paying bills, this may be a good option, but keep in mind that any time you give bank account information online, you are trusting that whoever has it will safeguard it. If their systems are hacked, your bank account information could be stolen. You'll want to weigh that risk against the convenience of automatic bill payment. Also, automatic bill payment does not mean you can "set it and forget it." You will need to make sure you keep good records of every payment made so that you can effectively balance your checkbook at the end of each month.

Balancing your checkbook is a task that is high importance, high urgency, and high in consequence. The act of balancing your checkbook is crucial for tracking your budget and expenditures. You need to know what you have available to spend. If you don't keep track on a regular basis, it will cost you money, because you may overdraw your bank account, or you may not catch when someone has made a mistake and charged you the wrong amount.

If you have a hard time with repetitive tasks like paying bills, you can take some steps to minimize this type of task by simply not incurring bills in the first place. You can do this by avoiding financing things and buying whatever you can outright. This may mean that you buy an older car for cash rather than lease a new car, or that you buy your Aunt Martha's old sofa instead of going to a fancy furniture store and taking them up on their 0 percent interest sale. This is a good strategy, for one, because it keeps your life simpler, and it keeps your costs down.

Housework

Housework can be a very personal thing. What works for each person may be different. The absolute bottom line is that you need to keep your house healthy. Leaving food around to rot, not cleaning up after animals, and not disposing of waste in a timely manner are all things that will make your house unhealthy. If it gets bad enough, neglecting these things can result in the ultimate high-consequence act: you could be evicted, or if you're living in a house, it could even be condemned.

When prioritizing tasks, pay special attention to anything that makes your house less safe, and factor into these considerations your particular health issues or challenges. For example, if you are profoundly allergic to dust or mold, then dusting or cleaning up mold will be much more important for you than it would be for someone else. Likewise, if you find coordination particularly difficult and you have a tendency to trip, then cleaning things up off the floor, and removing, straightening, or placing a rubber pad beneath loose throw rugs will be very important in order to avoid accidents. For the specific ins and outs of cleaning and housework, I rely upon a comprehensive book by Cheryl Mendelson, called *Home Comforts: The Art and Science of Keeping House.*

Keep a schedule, and make sure you include things like yearly tests of your smoke detectors. If you know the sound will bother you, wear earphones to muffle the sound. Make sure you have fire extinguishers in any room where cooking is done. Put rubber mats down in slippery bathtubs to prevent falls, and make sure you clean them regularly to avoid their becoming slimy from mildew.

Some adults on the spectrum have found a great deal of success with visual charts and setting up cleaning zones. For a better description of this than I could possibly get into here, see Zosia Zaks's book, *Life and Love: Positive Strategies for Autistic Adults.*

Personally, I have always coped by using technology, lists, and subtle visual prompts. First I make my list, prioritize the tasks using the matrix technique, and then I put them into a scheduling program, such as Microsoft Outlook or on my smartphone, so that I get reminders. If I need to move the task for any reason, I make sure to set a new date to take on that task. There are also advanced scheduler programs that will do this for you. One that particularly interests me is the PEAT system put out by Attention Control Systems, Inc. (*http://brainaid.com*). Developed by a former NASA robotics researcher, it was based on a computer model of human executive functions originally designed to make robots more autonomous. The model was specifically adapted for people with differences in attention and memory.

When I need to do a chore within the next few hours, sometimes I'll create a visual prompt by taking out something that I need in order to complete that task. For example, if I'm cooking dinner, and I remember that I need to do a load of laundry, I'll take out the laundry detergent and fabric softener, and put it somewhere in plain sight. This is a short, easy task that won't cause me to leave a hot stovetop unattended.

This technique becomes less and less effective the longer a task is postponed, because your perception gradually gets used to these two items being "out of place," and it doesn't perceive them as being out of place anymore. Since the effectiveness of the technique relies on the incongruity of the items because they are out of place, it no longer works as a reminder. This is why it's often good to set a reminder on your phone, or write down a reminder, so that you don't forget.

Building a Support System

In the safety chapter, we discussed strategic partnerships. The areas we've discussed so far in this chapter may also be good candidates for these partnerships. If you are living with a roommate, he may have skills that you lack, and you may have skills that he lacks. When you live with someone, talk about what you're good at and what she is good at, and see if you can find ways to break down tasks according to strengths and abilities. If there are some areas where you need additional help, you can have conversations like this with your friends and family as well. Find win-win scenarios.

If you don't know anyone who has a particular skill set, and you have enough money, you can hire someone to do those things. For example, there are a lot of services that specialize in basic cleaning or carpet cleaning. There are exchanges, such as *www.elance.com*, where you can find freelancers to help with particular projects. There are barter exchanges on sites like Craigslist. Or you could work out arrangements like this with your neighbors.

If you work out bartering situations with people you don't know, be very careful about the types of services you barter for, especially if it involves money (like errand running). They could take the money and disappear with it. If you are bartering, it's best to do it with someone you know well, or confine the barter to something that is concrete and does not open you to danger or crime. For more sensitive tasks, there are companies that will check a person's reputation, and even subject them to a background check. If you must outsource those tasks, it's best to pay money and go with a reputable company that can vouch for the person.

POINTS TO REMEMBER

- Choosing the right living arrangement will take a lot of planning.

- To begin the planning process, think about what you want to do, then put together a budget.

- Ideally, a roommate should be someone you know well; if not, make sure you interview potential roommates thoroughly.

- Be aware of the legalities of your rental or sublease agreement.

- One of the most important tasks in building a life that works is learning to prioritize what matters.

- Prioritize your tasks by their level of urgency, importance, and the severity of the consequences for not doing them.

- The most important purpose of housework is to keep your house safe and healthy for you to live in.

CHAPTER 6

Getting Around

Getting around. It's something many people take for granted, but for some of us it can be difficult. For those of us who have more difficulty getting around, it may take some additional planning for us to achieve the mobility we need. In this chapter, we'll talk about the safety of driving. Is it right for you? Under what circumstances? If you struggle, what can you do to expand your skills?

We'll also talk about alternatives to driving. What do you do if you're one of those who don't drive (or at least don't drive now)? Fortunately, there are options. We'll talk about them, and how they work. We'll discuss how to get a taxi, or how to find out about public transportation. We'll also talk about things like walking or riding a bike. When is it feasible? When does it provide an undue safety risk? We'll talk about all these things and how to handle them.

The Unexpected Consequences of Difficulties with Driving

One afternoon some years ago, my boss came to see me. Earlier that week, a program I had been running for the company had been chosen for an award by a national organization. The award ceremony was to be held at the White House, and the company was offered two tickets to the event. My boss had come to give me some news of his own—he wanted *me* to go along with an executive from another department. He was extremely excited, and I imagine he expected excitement and gratitude in return. But my initial reaction was anxiety.

Although by then I had some experiences with more formal work events, ceremonies, conferences, and the like, they were never easy for me. In fact, they were quite draining. And this wasn't just any conference or awards ceremony, this was *the White House*. While this could likely be a challenge for me, I didn't rule it out. Attending a function at the White House was no small thing. As nerve-racking as it might be, I wasn't willing to let fear of embarrassment be a reason to forgo such an opportunity.

I was close to agreeing when he continued. While I was there, he said, I could drive on over to Baltimore in order to meet with a business contact who had been elusive. I saw quite clearly that he seemed to expect this as a condition of participating. Unfortunately, this was something that slammed the door of opportunity closed with a reverberating "thud."

The expectation of a trip to Baltimore was a barrier I couldn't think my way through. My boss didn't know it, but I rarely drove to work. With some working around the company's travel policy, I might've been able to manage to attend the awards ceremony. Instead of renting a car, I could have used taxis and shuttles to get where I needed to go. That would leave only my sensory issues to deal with, and I hoped that I could find some creative ways around that.

But at the time, I did not feel comfortable speaking up about my challenges, fearing that my boss and others would be influenced by stereotypes associated with autism and have a lesser view of my capabilities. Looking at the diagnostic criteria, I feared that they might even assume that I couldn't successfully do my job, though that was clearly not the case.

My boss did not recognize my level of stress. On the contrary, he seemed to assume that I would say yes. Unfortunately, I was not conversationally quick enough to come up with something suitable to say. The more he talked, the more stressed I felt, feeling pressured into something I knew would be unsafe for me to do.

Finally, I burst out: "I'm not going to do it!" The stress, I knew, put an edge to my voice that certainly sounded ungracious. But I didn't know what to do about that. I felt that if I could have discussed my issues with him without fear of judgment, I might not have had to give up this opportunity. I resented being put in this situation where I felt like I had to choose between the opportunity of a lifetime and my own personal safety.

I took a lot of criticism for that choice from my manager, who put it in my review. He interpreted my abrupt response as ungratefulness, and my unwillingness to attend the function or go to Baltimore as a lack of commitment to my job in the company. It was a bitter lesson that taught me the difficulties that can be brought about by simple things like just getting around.

Nowadays, I'm much more straightforward with my boundaries. What I've learned in the time since is that people can't meet you where you are in terms of skills and abilities unless you communicate what those skills and abilities are. There are some who will be unduly judgmental, and who may challenge you. But there are also people who will surprise you with their willingness to adjust, *if* they know there's a need.

To Drive, or Not to Drive?

Driving can be difficult for some of us on the spectrum because of differences in attention and coordination. Perhaps you met this challenge when you reached the legal age to drive and regularly drive now, perhaps you have not yet considered it, or perhaps you had a negative experience with driving in the past and may consider it in the future. Only you can decide whether you feel it's a safe undertaking for you. What I learned about it was to take my time and learn at my own pace. Personally, I try never to say never with regard to learning new skills; however, I set very firm limits on my pace, especially when it's something like driving, which can have serious consequences. After you explore your abilities and perhaps take some classes, you may find that driving is not for you. There are a lot of people in this world who won't get that, but it's okay. Don't ever let anyone push you into doing something you know isn't safe for you to do just because they think you should be able to do it. Your safety comes first.

You may find, like I have, that driving works for you in specific situations but not in others. It can feel frustrating and limiting, but you must keep your safety in mind and be open to alternative solutions. What I have learned to do is to tell people, "I have trouble with freeway driving. I sometimes find it difficult to tell how far other cars are from me, so it's difficult and sometimes dangerous for me to do." No one is going to tell you that you need to put yourself in a situation that's unsafe, certainly not an employer who may fear being sued. Overall, I found that my coworkers take this fairly well and will go out of their way to offer up opportunities for carpooling to events and so forth. If that isn't possible, then we talk about alternative solutions.

When I park, I'm careful to try not to park next to another car, so that I have plenty of space while parking. If for some reason it is necessary for me to park in a place that makes me uncomfortable, I'll have someone act like an air traffic controller, to direct me correctly into the space.

When learning new skills, I've learned to practice when I am not under stress. It's often harder to retain a skill if you have practiced it only while on the edge of a meltdown. So if you do try to test your boundaries, practice under low-stress conditions over and over until you are comfortable. Then, little by little, try practicing that skill in a slightly more stressful environment, working up to an environment you might have found very frightening at the beginning. You may be surprised how far you can test your limits.

Public Transportation

If you cannot drive or can only drive under specific conditions, then you'll want to choose the location of your job and your home appropriately. If you choose to move into a place that isn't very accessible via public transportation, you may find that your job prospects are very limited.

Depending on the city you live in, the quality of your public transit system may vary. Some areas have very consolidated transit systems that involve buses, ferries, subways, and cable cars, which make it very easy to get to many areas. Many municipalities have websites where you can research bus routes and plan your route ahead of time. Google Maps now has public transportation as a setting, and you can put in two different locations in order to see how long it would take to get from one to the other, and the various ways you could do so using the transportation system.

If you're reliant on public transportation, keep track of changes to the schedule on weekends or holidays, and watch the news for any accidents or eventualities that may cause a delay in your chosen route. In some areas, buses and other forms of public transit have racks or other arrangements that allow you to bring your bike. Be prepared, though, in case the rack is full, or for some reason you get a bus that doesn't have one. Traveling via public transit can take longer and require more planning, but can be just as feasible as getting around via your own car.

In some cases, it allows you to be more productive than someone who has to drive, because on long rides you have plenty of time to read, write, or work. While riding on public transit, however, it's important to consider all of the safety precautions discussed in the safety chapter. Public transportation is one of the areas that is sometimes targeted by predators. So when you're in these areas, be very, very careful and aware of any suspicious behavior, and keep a tight grip on any valuables you may be carrying.

Other Options

There will be times when public transportation won't work for you. If you're going to the airport and have a lot of luggage, or if you're going shopping and will be bringing back a lot of groceries, you may want to consider taking a taxi or getting a ride with a friend or family member. In some cities, you can flag down a cab by waving at one. If they are in service, there is usually a light or a sign that tells you so. If that light is not on, that means that the cab driver isn't currently working and therefore will not stop. If you get frustrated that a taxi isn't stopping for you, *never* step out in front of one that's moving in an attempt to get it to stop.

If you need to be someplace at a particular time, then you're probably best off prearranging a taxi. Most taxi services have a phone number you can call to request a cab. If at all possible, you'll want to do this considerably ahead of time. If you put your order in a day before or hours before, the company's dispatcher can plan ahead to have a taxi in your area at the time you require; otherwise, you might face a delay.

It's customary to tip a taxi driver for good service. Standard amounts for tips may vary based on the area you're in. You may want to ask a family member or search online to find out what the recommended standard tip is in your area.

Other options for getting around can also include biking or walking. The safety of these two methods may depend on the time of day, the current weather, and the area you're traveling in. If you are traveling an area where motorists are not familiar or used to driving around bicycles, it can be more dangerous. If drivers don't know the proper etiquette, they may drive too closely to you, or cause you to have an accident. If that happens to you, you may want to consider riding on the sidewalk, even if it's technically not allowed. Be careful around pedestrians, but protect yourself as well.

It's also not a good idea to ride a bike or walk anywhere if it's dark. If you do, make sure you wear light-colored clothing, use a safety light or reflectors on your bike, or wear a jacket with reflectors on it. Also, it's best not to walk in an area where there aren't a lot of other people walking, if there isn't a sidewalk, or if houses or businesses are set too far back from the road to see you. If it's an area where people are not used to seeing someone walking, they may not handle it appropriately.

POINTS TO REMEMBER

- Only you can tell if driving is a safe activity for you. Never let anyone push you into doing something you know isn't safe. Your safety comes first.

- When trying a new driving skill, test it in a low-stress situation first, and then work up to higher-stress situations.

- If you don't drive, people may not understand, but it's okay.

- You may find you can drive, but only in certain situations.

- If confronted, you may want to disclose your difficulties, if it's clear people expect you to drive.

- If you know you'll be relying on public transportation, plan the location of your job and home accordingly.

- If you're riding a bike in an area where drivers aren't used to sharing the road with bicycles, you may need to ride on the sidewalk even if it isn't technically allowed.

- When walking, stick to well-trafficked areas that are well lit.

CHAPTER 7

Setting Career Goals

What do you want to do with your life? That's a big question, isn't it? That's why this is a big chapter. In it, we'll cover a lot. Planning for a career and finding a job is something that those on the autism spectrum struggle with, not only in theory, but also in implementation. In this chapter, we'll talk about some ways you can plan in order to have the best chances for success. We'll talk about the many online tools available to you in order to assess your fit for possible jobs (and their fit for you).

We'll discuss how to choose a job that will fit well with your skills, interests, and abilities, and we'll cover how to find out what credentials you need in order to get those jobs you are well suited for. We'll cover how to creatively figure out job opportunities that might be related to your special interests. We'll discuss resumes and cover letters. We'll talk about the type of research and preparation you'll need to do for an interview. We'll also cover disclosure —its risks and possible benefits. Finally, we'll talk about what happens after the interview and what to do when you get the call you've been seeking, one with the offer of a job!

A Career That Chose Me

Many people in the world seem to think that there is a particular path that you *need* to follow. You identify what you want to do with your life, figure out what skills you need, get the required experience and education, and get working. What so many people in this world learn is that, often, it's not that simple. Sometimes a career chooses you.

I struggled through much of my high school years trying to figure out what exactly I should target as a career path. I loved science, I loved to act, I enjoyed language, and I really enjoyed getting to know people of other cultures.

Combining the last two, I finally settled on the idea of being an interpreter. I was energized by learning new languages and was ambitious about the number of languages I would eventually master. Underneath it all, I think I saw my interest in language as being a way to expand my opportunities for friendship. After all, the more people you are able to talk to, the more people you could potentially connect with. I really didn't understand at that point that there was more to communication than just talking.

Then, a favorite teacher submitted a story of mine to a contest. It won and was published. Soon after, he came to see me to tell me that he had nominated me for a scholarship designed for students who were gifted in writing, using the award-winning story as an example of my work. When he came to tell me that I had won the scholarship, I was torn. I was set on being an interpreter. The news of the scholarship created a challenge.

I'll never forget the words my teacher said to me when he came to tell me that I'd won. "I don't know what you will do in life, precisely. But I'm convinced you'll do great things. And I'm even more convinced it'll have something to do with writing." Through all the twists and turns of my life since then, I found myself following a very different path than either my teacher or I would have hoped for.

Almost as an afterthought one day, when blogs were becoming increasingly popular, I decided to start one. After learning about my autism, I was trying to make sense of what it meant to me, especially looking back on my life. As I thought about it, I wondered if anyone would be helped by "listening in" on my process, through reading what I wrote. On that chance, I chose to make the blog public. Three years later, an editor stumbled across my blog, liked it, and invited me to blog for *Psychology Today*. That eventually led to this book.

I find myself humbled by the fact that my teacher was a better judge of my potential than I was. What it taught me is this: As sure as you may be about what you want to do with your life, sometimes the best opportunities come in areas you would never have thought of. And sometimes, other people see your potential far clearer than you do.

Planning Your Career

The first step in finding your career depends very much on the self-awareness we discussed in the first chapter of this book. To effectively identify the career that works best for you, you'll need to understand yourself, your abilities, your likes and dislikes, and what your goals are in life. Your ideal career will be dependent on all of these things.

What Do You Like to Do?

In most employment situations you'll be spending a great deal of time at work, so you want to choose something that excites you and that you would enjoy doing. This is where those of us who are on the autism spectrum may have a slight advantage, because so many of us know exactly what we like—it's part of the description of being a person with autism to have a deep and abiding interest in a particular topic or set of topics. The question is, how can you make money pursuing that interest?

Sometimes, the career you choose may be somewhat peripheral to that interest. For example, if your special interest is playing a particular video game, you're unlikely to find a career that is only about playing video games. But you may find careers or ways to make money that are somewhat related. If you have a good sense of how computers work, you could potentially pursue a degree in computer programming. You could potentially then come up with your own program, maybe one that's even better than the game you like!

In Our Own Words

Find a way to work with your special interest(s). These are areas you can become an expert in, and thus valuable. —Michael Bettine, Adult on the Autism Spectrum

If you're not good at computers, but you are good at writing, you could become a writer who focuses on developments in the video game industry. You could write for major magazines and online video game sites. Explore options and openings in the industry that interest you.

Other interests may make you marketable in a variety of industries. For example, my interest in languages might make me appealing to many international corporations, even those that are not directly involved in translating services.

These are just a few examples of ways in which you can look at your special interests for career ideas.

There are a lot of resources available at local libraries or at schools that will help you through this process. The Myers-Briggs test, which we discussed earlier in this book, and tests like it, are often administered in schools as a way of identifying potential career goals. In addition, there are many books on the jobs available in specific industries, what skill sets and education they require, and the types of working environments and conditions you can expect.

One that is particularly useful is the *Occupational Outlook Handbook*, published by the Bureau of Labor Statistics. Some libraries may have a print version, but it is now primarily a web publication, which can be accessed at *www.bls.gov/ooh/*. The site provides lists of the highest paying jobs, the most in demand jobs, as well as profiles of different industries and jobs within them. For individual jobs, it will show you the median salary, and the typical education and skills required for that job.

There are also many great books on the process of career planning. The most popular and well known is the book *What Color Is Your Parachute?* by Richard Bolles. This book is rewritten and published every year with new information tailored to the current job market. It's a great book to give you a basic framework regarding how to identify your skills and abilities, assess potential career options, and how to find jobs in your chosen field.

Some schools may have a career counselor available to help students identify appropriate careers. If not, you might find it helpful to hire one privately. For more information on how to find the right one, visit the National Career Development Association (*http://ncda.org*).

Assessing Your Own Abilities

One thing to be cautious about when you're thinking about the type of career you want to pursue is to make sure that you are basing your decision on your *own* assessment of your abilities and strengths, versus solely on a diagnosis or a set of test scores. While these kinds of things can be helpful in your decision-making process, try not to let them limit you too much. Remember that you, and your abilities, are unique. A set of diagnostic criteria, or a score on a test, may indicate general patterns amongst a group of people, but it does not necessarily represent a true picture of your overall abilities. Theory and reality are two different things.

In Our Own Words

What you *want* to do, and what you're *able* to do, may be entirely different. Your ideal career may not even remotely resemble what your aptitude tests claimed you should do. —Ennien Ashbrook

Some adults on the spectrum have received test scores or consulted career coaches who told them that there is a very specific and narrow list of careers that they are suited for, yet when they went out into the workplace, they found that their aptitude and successful, real life career experience was in a completely different field. You may also find success in fields that aren't typically considered for a person with autism.

For example, there are many who will tell you that those on the autism spectrum should never be a manager. For some people, and in some situations, this is absolutely appropriate. These recommendations were clearly based on input from people who had been unsuccessful in such a role. However, there are some who have been successful in this type of a position, despite the challenges that being on the spectrum can present. Malcolm Johnson, an adult on the autism spectrum, wrote an entire book on the subject, called *Managing with Asperger Syndrome*.

It's important to make your own decisions based on your own goals, your own strengths, and what you feel that you can handle. The greater autism community tends to focus on deficits, what we can't do, versus what we can. Because of this, it may be tempting to limit yourself more than you need to.

When you are considering potential careers, only you can decide whether the particular challenges that you encounter or expect to encounter warrant changing your career goals. What benefit would pursuing that particular career path bring you? Would the challenges you face diminish those benefits? Or are there ways of creatively overcoming those challenges in ways that people haven't previously considered? What will it cost you to pursue that career path, in terms of effort, strength, and stress? Will you be required to work so hard to overcome your challenges that you'll be exhausted at the end of every day? Will the stress drive you into meltdowns or affect your health? After having considered all of this, do you think that the benefits are greater than the potential costs? Most of all, considering all of the requirements of the job and your abilities (with or without accommodations), will you be able to be effective enough in the job to survive in a competitive environment?

Finding Job Opportunities

Finding a job can be one of the more difficult aspects of the workplace, especially for those of us on the spectrum. For better or for worse, some of the most effective ways of finding a job, according to statistics, are techniques that are social in nature. While many of us think about job hunting in terms of reading through classified ads in the newspaper, statistics show that as many as 85 percent of jobs are found through networking or other social means. In other words, most jobs are found through talking to people.

This may make you anxious. However, there are a number of ways you can go about making this easier for you. First of all, make sure you understand clearly what your value proposition is. When I say "value proposition," I mean what is it that you have to offer employers that they need. Determining this may require some research, such as looking through the profiles in the *Occupational Outlook Handbook*, talking to people in the industry, or reading books and articles about trends in your chosen field. Take a look particularly at what you have to offer that other people don't.

When an employer is considering hiring a prospective employee, she will look at what she's expecting to gain from the position, and then weigh each candidate's skills and abilities against those expectations. She may not write it out on paper, but in her mind, she will have a list of qualities she wants in a candidate, as well as qualities she doesn't want in a candidate. You want to be able to demonstrate that you have more of the qualities that she wants, and fewer of the qualities she doesn't want. And it helps if you have a demonstrable skill or ability that impresses her enough that she adds a new requirement to the list of qualities she wants.

Even before you find or apply for a job, you'll want to make sure you have a good sense of what you have to offer, and be able to articulate that well to a potential employer. This will help you in the interview phase of the employment process, which we will talk about in the next chapter, but will also help you in the job search process. First of all, it will help you in writing good cover letters, and in formulating your resume. Second, you will need to put together an "elevator speech" that you can use with prospective employers. It is called an elevator speech because it is a short description of yourself and what you offer an employer that you could quickly state in a short encounter, such as an elevator ride.

This last point is particularly important because, as previously mentioned, many of the jobs that are available you will find via networking. This means talking with someone in an elevator, or talking to a friend of your parents, or a friend of a friend. You need to be able to speak to a number of people about the type of job you want and quickly convey why you would be good at it and what an employer will gain by hiring you.

Job Sites and Listings

Once you have developed a good "elevator speech," then you'll be better prepared for the next step—which is starting the search. In order to maximize your chances for success, you'll want to use a number of techniques to identify potential opportunities. First of all, there are more traditional, "passive" techniques, such as browsing online job listings and offline publications, such as newspapers or trade journals. Nowadays, online job searching is so common that there are many places you can find such listings. There are generic job listing sites:

- *www.monster.com*

- *www.vault.com*

- *www.indeed.com*

- *www.simplyhired.com*

There are also specialty job boards:

- *www.dice.com* (for jobs in the technology industry)

- *www.usajobs.gov* (for jobs in the federal government)

- *http://stylecareers.com* (for jobs in the fashion industry)

- *www.allretailjobs.com* (for jobs in the retail business)

- *www.healthecareers.com* (for jobs in the health care industry)

These sites can easily be found by searching on Google for keywords like "job boards," or "job search," and using these terms along with keywords related to your specialty to find specific sites in your field. These sites aggregate listings for multiple employers in one place and can be a good place to start.

Although these sites often have a lot of listings, they will not include every possible listing for every possible employer. So you may want to go to specific employers' websites and look there. Most companies that are large enough will have one.

Depending on the nature of the type of work that you want to do, you may be able to read through trade magazines and journals, or search on the Internet, to find out who the top employers are in a specific field. You can also ask friends, family, or mentors with knowledge of your particular industry of interest. In the process you'll also want to think about the type of company you would like to work for in terms of culture. Do you want to work in a company that is innovative and creative and that lets people think creatively? Or would you prefer a working environment that's very rules-based, and therefore, predictable? Also look to "best of" lists, books, and websites for information on the work environment at a specific company.

Referrals and Networking

As discussed earlier in this chapter, statistics show that most jobs are not found via searching through job listings or classified ads. For us, this particular technique might seem easier on the surface because it doesn't initially require social contact. Unfortunately, when you go through a job site or apply to an ad, this usually forces you into a hiring infrastructure that is typically stacked against people on the spectrum.

Most job applications and resumes received through such a process will be directed straight to HR (human resources). HR professionals are trained specifically to screen resumes and applicants. Unfortunately, many of the typical ways that they screen might have a disparate effect on someone on the spectrum. For example, they may exclude a candidate who doesn't appear to be enthusiastic on the telephone. This could lead to candidates being excluded who have an unusual speaking style, or who might sound "monotone," regardless of their real level of enthusiasm regarding the job.

For better or for worse, hiring an employee is often a social process. Employers want to *know* the person they are hiring. They want to understand not only the person's skill set, but how he goes about doing their job. In most of the places I've worked in, the majority of people who are successfully hired were people who were referred to the hiring manager directly by someone who had worked with before or who knew that person personally. Employers want to know that what you have represented in your marketing materials (your resume and cover letter) are really as advertised.

Because of this, one of the very important tools you'll need to have at your disposal in your job search process is a list of references and their contact information. These are people who know you and can provide perspective on the type of person you are. Ideally, a reference should be someone who is not related to you, who can appear at least somewhat objective. If you give references such as family members or a boyfriend or girlfriend, they will have less weight with the employer, because the employer will be concerned that they will be biased toward saying positive things about you.

Always make sure that you have a person's permission prior to using him or her as a reference and ask about giving out personal information, such as an e-mail or phone number. Some people prefer not to give this information to people they don't know. If you give out such information without their approval, they will likely be very unhappy and thus will not give you a good reference.

You'll also want to make sure that the people serving as your reference are aware that they will be receiving a call from the prospective employer. You'll want them to be prepared when the potential employer calls, and it's always a good idea to give them some idea of the job and the things that the employer has stated, either in the interview or in the job description, as being important. This gives the person acting as a reference the opportunity to choose her comments very specifically to highlight your capabilities and traits that are important to the employer.

Sometimes, you might get very lucky to find out that someone you or your family knows is hiring for a job. This is helpful because this employer already knows you, and if your skills and personality traits are a good match for what he's looking for, you may have an advantage over someone whom he does not know. The key thing is to find out when acquaintances may be hiring. This may not happen unless you make it known that you are looking for a job. Because of this, it's a good idea to have a few short scripts to use when you see friends, acquaintances, or friends of the family. It's usually not best to ask them about a job immediately; observe some common pleasantries first. You want to make sure to say, "Hello," ask how they are, and employ the type of small talk that you would use in any other situation.

If they ask you a question about how you are doing, or what you're "up to" these days, that's a good transition to bring up the subject. You can say something like, "I am doing well. I've been doing (typical activities you enjoy). Also, I'm looking for a job in (your chosen field). I'm just at the beginning of the search, and have a few leads, but still nothing firm. If you happen to know anyone who's looking for someone in that area, I'd really appreciate it if you'd pass on my information." If they know someone who might have an opening, they may volunteer that person's name right then, if not, they may get back to you later. They may also ask you to tell them about yourself, or your qualifications. This is a good time to use your elevator speech. You want to convey the basics of your skills and qualifications in a concise and direct way that they can remember. This way, they'll be likely to remember more of it, in the event that they need to repeat the information later to a prospective employer.

One tool that can help you in the networking process is LinkedIn (*www.LinkedIn.com*). This is a site that is almost a cross between Facebook and a job listings site. On LinkedIn, you fill out a profile highlighting your own skills and abilities, something very similar to your resume, and you connect to the people you know. This allows you to more concretely see what your network looks like. Your "network" is the community of people whom you know directly, whom they know, and whom those people know. It multiplies fairly quickly. The plus side of sites like LinkedIn is that you can easily find out what your network looks like by looking at the profile of different friends and acquaintances, and you can conduct this type of networking in a more structured way. In offline networking, you would simply talk to someone about your job interests, and hope that she thought of the friend of a friend who works at the company where you want to work.

Another place where you can connect with people in your industry is by joining online and offline groups of people that share your interests. Some industries have organizations that sponsor "mixers" or other events. If you're not comfortable with in-person socializing, there are many online trade groups that you can join. LinkedIn has a number of these around different interests and industries. There are also different groups that are for people of certain demographic groups, such as professional women, members of ethnic minorities, and those who have disabilities. If you look for them, there are groups for people on the autism spectrum. These groups provide ways to make connections with others who have faced those challenges and navigated through them successfully.

If you need help with LinkedIn, online searches return thousands of book titles that have been written on how to use LinkedIn effectively, and there are a number of good online sources as well. There is an entire site, Linked Intelligence, that's dedicated to such advice (*http://linkedintelligence.com*). The About.com Job Searching site (*http://jobsearch.about.com*) and Lifehacker (*http://lifehacker.com*) have also put together good articles and advice on using LinkedIn.

When it comes to networking, it's tempting to simply focus very narrowly on getting a job and getting it now. However, networking doesn't always work that way. If a contact doesn't have a job open that you can apply to, it's still important to think of that person as a resource. Once a contact knows your skills and abilities, he may contact you at a later date. Or he may be a possible mentor for you, a person who could give you advice and guidance to help you get through difficult situations. This only happens, however, if you build a relationship, rather than simply looking at this person as a means to a goal.

When someone gives you the name of an acquaintance or a friend of a friend who might be able to help you, but whom you're not sure will have a job opening, it's still a good idea to contact that person. First of all, *he* may know somebody who has a job opening that would fit what are looking for. Second of all, if he has experience in your industry or within a company that you would like to work for, he may have valuable expertise to share with you—the kind of expertise you can't learn in a classroom. In those instances, you may want to contact the person and ask him for an informational interview.

This is typically a very short meeting or call with the person, where you ask her to share some of her experiences with you. If she works at a company that you're thinking about working for, you can ask her about what it is like working for that company. What is the company culture like? These can be very important questions for people on the spectrum, as certain cultures are not always welcoming toward those on the autism spectrum. If the person has the job that you would like to be doing, or has had that job in the past, this can be a great opportunity to ask her for advice on how to land that job, and how to be successful in that role. Ask her what she likes about her job and what she doesn't like about her job. For additional advice in this area, which is written specifically with an adult on the autism spectrum in mind, you can also read the book, *Developing Talents: Careers for Individuals with Asperger Syndrome and High-Functioning Autism* by Temple Grandin and Kate Duffy.

Agencies and Recruitment Companies

Another way that you can go about looking for a job is by working with recruiters or temporary agencies. Recruitment companies and temporary agencies work in different ways, but what they have in common is that they both assist employers to find candidates for open jobs. There are different types of recruiters, but what differentiates them from the temporary agency or a contract agency is that the jobs that they are most often recruiting for are primarily full-time permanent positions, whereas temporary agencies and contract agencies are often brought on by an employer to find help for a short-term need. The first is very similar to working with an employer, but here are some details you should know about working with a temporary agency (often referred to as "temp agencies").

If you are in the phase of your career where you are gaining experience and/or need an interim job while you are in school, working with agencies like this may be a valid approach. Most of these agencies will test your skills and abilities before they even do an interview with you. If you have particularly strong gifts in a particular area, this can be helpful because you are highlighting your skills first, then dealing with the social challenge of the interview second.

If you have particular skills to offer, can prove those skills via skills testing, and you can present yourself as a reliable, hardworking employee, working for temporary agencies can be a good choice to get experience. Many people who work for temporary agencies don't take it seriously, and so those who are willing to take those jobs and treat them with the same discipline as a "regular" job will be first on the list to be called for the next job opening.

Temping positions as a career route may not work for everyone, but it can be a viable option for some. There are benefits and drawbacks to it that really depend on each person's individual situation. If you prefer predictability, and would want to go to work at the same place every day and do the same thing, it would not be a good option for you. If you need health insurance, you may have to look very carefully at the agency you are working with to see what they have available. Some high-end agencies provide all the same benefits as a full-time employer, while some do not.

Temp agencies are paid by "marking up" your hourly or weekly pay. This means that they may charge the employer a great deal more than they are paying you. These rates can be very different depending on your industry, the agency, and the contract they have negotiated with the company where you work. They take this payment in order to cover their administrative costs, such as payroll management, drug tests, other testing, etc. What this means is that you may have the potential to make more money in the beginning if you seek full-time permanent employment directly with a hiring company instead of going through an agency. This of course depends on whether the company would be willing to hire you directly or not.

Working as a contractor or freelancer may be nontraditional, but if you like it, can make a steady income at it, and it works for you, don't let people make you feel bad about it.

Volunteering and Internships

When employers evaluate your resume, they will look for your experience in a workplace. Not having that can be a drawback. This may seem unfair, but it is true. Many employers want to see experience before you get a job, but you need a job in order to get experience. This is where volunteering and internships can potentially be useful.

There are volunteer opportunities in many different areas, and duties can be wide-ranging: taking photos, training people to use computers or setting them up, auctioning products on the Internet, painting buildings or doing maintenance, or even writing communications for a charity. Whatever you're good at, there is likely some organization that needs that type of service.

While you won't get paid, volunteering will help you to get experience and demonstrate your skills to others. If you prove yourself to be reliable, the people you work with at the charity may even become references for you when you do apply for a paid job.

In addition, it's a way of being involved in giving back to the community. To find volunteer opportunities, you can look at some of the charities in your area. You can look particularly at charities that are related to an area you're interested in. If you're not sure which charities are around, or which ones would have need for your skills, there are also volunteering search sites that will let you search by the type of duties involved or your skills:

- *www.volunteermatch.org*

- *http://smartvolunteer.org*

- *www.serve.gov*

- *www.idealist.org*

- *www.volunteer.gov*

Each of these sites has search interfaces that allow you to search for an opportunity that you think would work out well for you.

Internships are low-paying or unpaid opportunities to work in a company in order to learn about the company and gain experience. Internships are primarily offered to students or recent graduates. Some may even get academic credit for their time spent as an intern. Internships can often be very competitive, especially in academic or very specialized fields, but they can provide opportunities for exposure to what the workplace and industry are really like, to build contacts, and to show your abilities. In many organizations, interns that perform well have a very good chance of being hired later for a full-time, paid position.

Just like volunteering, internships are available in a wide variety of industries, covering a wide breadth of skill sets. A major museum may offer internships for those interested in natural history, a botanical garden may offer internships for someone studying horticulture, or a major accounting firm may offer an internship for a student studying accounting. You can often find out about available internships through academic advisers, career fairs, and other school resources. But there are also online listings for internships as well:

- *www.internweb.com*

- *http://internships.com*

- *http://college.monster.com/education*

- *http://internjobs.com*

Agencies for People with Disabilities

In many areas, there are public agencies specifically designed to find jobs for people with disabilities. The way these agencies operate can vary widely based on their locality, so it is difficult to generalize. The feedback I have received on such agencies has been mixed, but it is a conduit that's worth exploring, if you feel it would be a good fit. Certainly, the extreme diversity of the clientele they serve provides a challenge to the agency and may affect your experience with them. The needs of a person who uses a wheelchair, the needs of someone with PTSD, the needs of someone who has a visual impairment, and the needs of someone with an intellectual disability are all very different from one another. Many agencies may have more experience with these types of disabilities than they may have with autism. Because of this they may find it very difficult to understand how to support someone on the autism spectrum. If you are interested in seeing how such an agency could help you, it may be a good idea to ask them how many people on the autism spectrum they have been able to place in jobs, and how many of them were still working at that job a year later. This may give you a sense of how effective they are at placing those on the autism spectrum versus those with other disabilities.

Self-Employment

Many adults on the spectrum have found that self-employment is a good option for them. If you are self-employed, you can design your work space, schedule, and duties to your particular profile of strengths and abilities. However, there are also additional responsibilities. It may require resources in terms of money for start-up expenses, equipment, and additional tax obligations. To protect yourself, you'll want to make sure that you learn as much as you can about tax law and laws regarding running a business. Some industries, such as construction, require you to obtain special licensing and may subject you to very expensive fines if you attempt to work in that field without those licenses. There are resources available, however, to help entrepreneurs with disabilities to get started.

Disability.gov (*www.disability.gov*), a service of the government, provides specific guidance and information for people with disabilities who want to start their own business. Another useful site is the one for the Small Business Administration (*www.sba.gov*). The SBA is a division of the government that is responsible for supporting and encouraging the success of small businesses in the United States. On this site you'll learn how to write a business plan, how to get funding or grants, business law, and best practices for successfully running a business.

The SBA also has local offices in most cities, and there are Small Business Development Centers throughout the United States that provide support and assistance. To find your local SBDC, visit the Association of Small Business Development Centers online at *www.asbdc-us.org*. Click on the "Resources" link for a wealth of information for those who are trying to start a business.

Finally, a great organization to seek out for help in establishing your business is the Service Corps of Retired Executives, otherwise known as SCORE. This is a group of retired executives from the business world who volunteer their time to mentor entrepreneurs in the process of developing a successful business. Their website is *www.score.org.*

If you decide to pursue self-employment, you will need to develop discipline and strong organizational skills in order to plan your time appropriately. You will not have a boss or other person dictating tasks to you, so you will need to be able to effectively prioritize the tasks necessary for completing the work in order to fulfill your obligations. Make sure you have a full understanding of what this work will be, including the administrative tasks required in running your own business.

A second point to consider is that even if you are self-employed, many of the skills discussed in this chapter will still apply. In fact, you may need to develop these skills to an even greater extent than if you were simply just looking for a job. Whereas someone who's looking for a "regular" job will need to go through the processes we've discussed primarily only when he is searching for a new job, in many self-employment business situations, you will need to do this very frequently.

For you to be successful, you will need to find customers on a regular basis, which requires many of the same skills as does looking for a job. Most small business owners are constantly looking for new customers, and in many industries, that means almost constant networking. So when you consider self-employment, try to consider all the different aspects of what self-employment entails. If the benefits outweigh the negatives, then it might be the right way to go for you.

Assessing Potential Job Opportunities

Once you have found a job listing you are interested in, be careful not to take the text in a listing too literally. When an employer is looking to fill a position, they are typically looking for a few key skills or traits. Unfortunately, most job descriptions do a very poor job of letting you know what those particular skills and traits are. The descriptions of those skills may be written in a way that is not clear, using terms that are not relevant to anyone outside the organization, or outside the industry. In addition, descriptions may include "fluff" content. These are traits and bullet points that are included in just about every job description, whether crucial to your success in the job or not. For example, a job description for a computer programmer may read that you must be able to lift 95 pounds, because that's included in all the company's job descriptions. When you're reading the job description, try to determine which of the skills and traits listed would be crucial for success in the job. Looking at the job descriptions and comparing it to more generic descriptions of that job may help in this process.

For example, you might look up the job title in the *Occupational Outlook Handbook* and read the "How to Become One" section for that occupation, which describes the necessary education, training, certification, or licenses to get a job in that occupation. At the bottom of that section, there is a summary of the most important qualities and skills required for the job. If these qualities and skills match up with skills mentioned in the job description, these are likely key points for the employer. Other skills may have less weight in terms of whether you'll be considered. Keep in mind, also, that some of the terms used in job descriptions can be ambiguous. For example, many job descriptions cite "communication skills" as a criterion, but this phrase means something very different when included in a job description for a vice president in a *Fortune* 500 corporation than it does in a job description for a computer programmer.

When you see skills like that listed, try to think about what they might mean in the context of the rest of the job. Communication skills can be broken down into a lot of sub-skills, and the employer may be looking for different combinations of these sub-skills. "Communication skills" could mean "the ability to come up with a strategy for achieving a project, persuading others of the benefits of that strategy, and communicating clearly to employees what it takes to accomplish it," or it could be as simple as "being able to tell someone how a program you coded works." It won't always be clear to you which the employer means, until you get to talk to them in person.

Because of this, don't be too intimidated to apply for a job if you see something like this in a job description. When in doubt, and you have the majority (or most important) skills called for, go ahead and apply. The surest way not to get a job is not to apply for it in the first place.

Your First Job Versus Your Dream Job

In my early years, I learned that in order to survive, I sometimes had to face the fact that I had to get "the best job for now," instead of "the best job ever." Early in my career, I took a number of entry-level jobs. I worked second shift (late evening to early morning) in the post office sorting mail, did manual labor, acted as a courier in a hospital, researched warranty claims, answered phones at a car dealership, worked in a call center, and many other roles.

None of these jobs was my ideal job, but I can definitely say that I learned something from each one of them. Eventually, the experience I learned in these jobs allowed me to get into the role

I have today. What many of us on the spectrum have learned is that just because a job isn't your ideal job doesn't mean that it isn't a good job. Sometimes, an interim job will lead you into an even better job than you had previously hoped for. But it does require patience.

In Our Own Words

Don't expect to start in your ideal job. As long as there is opportunity for advancement where you are, be the best at what you do, make friends, be likeable, help others, and you will not only have fun, but you will be given more responsibility and you will work your way up the ladder. —Michael F. Wilcox, Autistic Adult

In most industries, you'll need to start in a lower-level position and work yourself into a job with more responsibility. This period is designed for you to learn how to apply what you've learned in school or in previous jobs, which can be challenging. One mistake that many make when they're in these roles is to be arrogant and have the attitude that the job is stupid or not worth your time. Look at every job, no matter how menial you might think it is in that moment, as a learning experience. Every job is one you can put on your resume, and every supervisor is a possible future reference.

If you are in college or just coming out of college, you have already made the choice to obtain higher education. If you are in high school or just graduating, this is an issue you'll have to consider in your career planning process. What you would like to do with your life will have a strong impact as to how much education you pursue. As you research possible careers, you'll see in job descriptions and in the *Occupational Outlook Handbook* that there are some jobs for which a certain level of education is required.

If your chosen field requires a university education, this may require some additional planning on your part. You may not be able to go directly into this field until you are able to complete a certain level of education. If you do not have the resources to attend college without having a job, you will probably need an interim job, which may or may not be in the field in which you ultimately desire to work. When you choose an interim job for this reason, you'll need to assess what time and resources you'll need to successfully keep up with your classes, so that you can assess the time and schedule that you have available for the job.

In college towns, there are often more jobs available that provide you the flexibility necessary for you to maintain your studies. In other areas, it may be a little more difficult. This need for flexibility may make it more difficult to find a job in your particular field. This may be a disappointment, but it is sometimes a fact. If you are in this situation, then you'll want to make sure that you maintain the right attitude toward your interim job.

Preparing to Apply for a Job

In order to apply on any job site, you'll need a good resume, or curriculum vitae (CV), as it's known in some areas. This is, in essence, your "marketing document" that summarizes to an employer your skills, job history, education, and abilities, and the value you can bring to an organization. Typically, a beginning resume should be no longer than one page. There are too many considerations on how to design your resume to get into them in detail here, but there are many resources available on how to do this, both online and offline.

The About.com Job Searching website provides a number of samples of the different types of formats you can use, as well as articles regarding how to write and design an effective resume. There are also many books that provide examples and tips on how to write a good resume. One that I've referenced a great deal is a book called *Knock 'em Dead Resumes, 10th Edition: How to Write a Killer Resume That Gets You Job Interviews.* It's a good book, but does use a great deal of idioms (as you might see from the title).

If you visit your local bookstore or library, or search your favorite online bookstore, you'll probably find one that works for you. I have typically found that it helps to review a few different books. Different writers sometimes have slightly different opinions about how to design a resume, what to include, and how to write it. By referencing a few different books, you may find that some present the information in a way that makes better sense to you than do others.

You'll also need to have what is known as a *cover letter.* This is a letter that serves to introduce you, your skills, and your resume. Typically, you would tailor this cover letter to each particular job you're applying to, at least when that is possible. Just as covered above for resumes, the About.com Job Searching site also has a section on how to write cover letters and a number of sample cover letters. In addition, there are many books that can provide guidance on the subject. One example is the book *Winning Letters That Overcome Barriers to Employment: 12 Quick and Easy Steps to Land Job Interviews* by Daniel Porot and Frances Bolles Haynes. You could also try *Knock 'em Dead Cover Letters, 10th Edition: Cover Letter Samples and Strategies You Need to Get the Job You Want.* As with resumes, I find that seeking out a number of different books on the subject is most helpful.

If you have trouble with spelling, ask someone who is good at it to help you by reviewing your resume. It is very important to make sure your resume is error free and complete.

Always follow the company's directions for sending a resume and cover letter when applying for a job. Many job search sites ask you to upload your cover letter and resume into the website itself. In other instances, you'll be expected to e-mail or even send them in the mail. If you are selected to go to an interview, it's a good idea to have a paper version of your resume with you. This way, if the interviewer forgets his copy of the resume, you'll be prepared with a copy to provide him. When you're providing a paper copy that you printed, it's more professional to provide the documents on higher-quality paper, often called "resume paper."

Another detail that you'll want to pay attention to is the contact information you provide on the cover letter and resume. Make sure that the e-mail address that you use is one that is more generic. Definitely avoid an e-mail address that has any words in it that might be considered off-color, profane, or offensive. This isn't the place for amusing e-mail addresses. Having such an e-mail address on your cover letter or resume will cause most employers to consider you unprofessional and will get you very quickly removed from consideration. The best option is an e-mail address that is comprised of your name. In instances where your name is common and someone has already reserved the e-mail address of the same name, you can simply add a number to the end, punctuation such as a period or underscore, or some other identifying text, such as a state abbreviation. You want something that an employer will easily recall. Don't use your e-mail address with your current employer, if you have one. This will also often get you excluded from consideration, as it shows that you are using company time and resources for personal reasons. The prospective employer will wonder if you would do the same if they were to hire you.

The second important piece of contact information you need to keep in mind is the phone number you provide. Is it a private phone number, or is it shared with others? Can you trust that the others who share this telephone number will pass on messages to you reliably? Also, what will prospective employers hear if they called the number and reach a voice mail message? Will it be something generic such as, "Hello, this is _____. I'm not available at the moment, but please leave a message after the tone and I'll get back to you as soon as possible."? Or is it a recording of you singing a dirty limerick? The first is more likely to get you interviewed. If you have trouble with the telephone, or cannot speak on the telephone, make sure you provide instructions on how the employer can reach you successfully. For example, if you have trouble hearing on the phone, do you use a TTY service or a telephone captioning service? If so, provide the information for contacting you via this service and instructions on how to do so on the cover letter or resume. If you cannot use the phone at all, then indicate this on the cover letter or resume and provide your preferred method of contact. As with e-mail, make sure that you use your own phone number and not an employer's. Once again, potential employers will have concerns if it is clear to them that you are utilizing your current employer's time and equipment for your job search.

POINTS TO REMEMBER

- A good place to start the thinking about a possible career is within your special interests.

- To assess whether a job is a good fit, research it and ask questions of mentors. Be prepared for the fact that some jobs sound good in a book but may not work well in reality.

- If you decide that a job would not be a good fit for you, make sure that decision is based on your *own* assessment of your suitability and not solely based on the projections of others or on test scores.

- There are many ways to find a job, but the most effective methods are based on networking with others.

- Always have a short "elevator speech" ready to describe your skills and abilities, and the type of job you are seeking.

CHAPTER 8

Interviewing for Jobs

Ideally, the product of all this work will result in a request for an interview with a prospective employer. The purpose of an interview is to help you and the potential manager assess if you will be a good fit for the job. From your standpoint, your job in the interview will be to represent your skills and abilities in the most positive, yet accurate way. The interviewer's job is to ask you questions and try to determine from your answers to those questions, and how you conduct yourself in the interview, if you will be the best candidate for the job.

Really wanting a job (or really *needing* a job) can be very anxiety provoking to begin with. This pressure can make job interviews very stressful for just about anyone, neurotypical people included. But, it's important to remember that if you're being called for an interview, that's a good thing. The fact that you have been called means you've done something right. Your resume was interesting enough that they want to learn more about you.

Preparing for the Interview

Now, you need to prepare for the interview. Because so much is dependent on how you appear to the employer in the interview, you'll want to do whatever is necessary to make yourself appear in the best light possible. First, you'll want to prepare for the most common interview questions. You can't predict for sure what questions an interviewer will ask so it's best if you prepare memorized scripts for many of the most common questions. If you search for "most common interview questions" on the Internet, you'll find many examples of these common questions as well as sample responses that you can adapt to fit your own situation.

After you've spent some time planning your scripts, you'll want to practice them. You want to have these responses memorized and practiced to the extent that they come automatically. You'll also want to rehearse several variations of these answers, in case you get slightly different questions from different interviewers, and so that you can vary your answers between different interviewers at the same company. Interviewers will talk to one another after the interview. If you gave the same answer verbatim to every interviewer, they may pick up on that and think that your responses are less sincere. (Amongst those with a neurotypical makeup, a thought-out answer is often perceived as less genuine or sincere, because it can be so much easier for them to access and decode their own thoughts and feelings quickly. The perception is that if you delay your response, you're doing so because you're thinking of how to say what you don't really feel or think.)

My experiences in the theater gave me a big advantage when I began interviewing. For me, the skills for interviewing are very similar to the skills it takes to go out on stage. First, you memorize the script (but leave some room for ad libs). Second, you rehearse the script (hopefully with someone who can prompt you when you miss lines, and give you overall feedback on your performance). Third, incorporate feedback, practicing over and over again, until the dialog feels so natural it's automatic to you. Fourth, perform the event!

In Our Own Words

Practice out loud. Time yourself if you're an over talker, like I am. —Susie R.

If you are lucky enough to have someone in your life who can and will help you practice, it can be invaluable. If not, you might consider seeing if you can find someone who could provide this service for you. If you're coming out of college, perhaps your college's career counseling office could refer you to someone who could help you in this area. This is also something that a career counselor or interview coach may be able to help you with. Keep in mind, however, that such services can be costly.

When you practice, make sure you practice nonverbal communication as well, to the extent that you are able. Practice skills like giving a firm handshake. Since eye contact is what communicates to a neurotypical person that you are paying attention to her, try practicing it, if it isn't too uncomfortable, while you're running through the interview questions with a partner or coach. Ask for feedback on length of eye contact, and remember to break eye contact periodically. Making eye contact that is too prolonged will make the interviewer uncomfortable.

If you feel you cannot make eye contact, try to look at her forehead, or at an area near her eyes. If that is too difficult, or eye contact is simply not an option for you, practice a disclosure statement indicating why you aren't looking the interviewer in the eyes. If making eye contact while you are still learning the scripts is overwhelming, then break the whole process down into steps. Work on your scripts until you are comfortable with them, and then move on to practicing them along with the eye contact and body language.

Putting Company Research to Work for You

During the interview, many employers may ask you questions about your knowledge of their company. Be prepared to answer these questions. If you were thorough in searching for job opportunities, you'll already have a lot of this information. It's a good idea, when you are going through that initial research, to take notes about what you read about that company. Then, when you are preparing for your interview, you can refer to these notes in order to come up with scripted answers to some of the standard questions in this area.

Some of these questions will be general, such as, "Tell me, what do you know about our company?" To be prepared for questions like this, you can review the company's website in order to learn about the breadth of products and services they offer. If you're interviewing for a job in a financial area with a public company, having some knowledge of their financial status through reading their annual report and/or 10-K is a good idea. It will be even better if you can memorize some of the facts you find as well as understand them enough to make comments about them. This can help you to turn some of the interviewer's questions into questions of your own. This is helpful because coming up with good questions to ask the interviewer is often a challenge for many people, but doing so is expected by most interviewers.

Ask questions that demonstrate the depth of the research you have done, that show you comprehend the information that you researched, and that provoke an answer from the interviewer that will likely tell you something about who he or she is. Does he give you just general answers, or does he answer you directly and honestly? If he is bound by company policy not to comment, is he honest about that? Although these things are small, they may give you an indication of how this person may be as a manager, which is an important consideration for you if you are eventually offered the position.

In Our Own Words

A company [representative] likes to really hear, and see, and have validated that an applicant has actually done some homework on the company. —Michael John Carley

Another version of this question that the interviewer may ask you is, "Why are you interested in working at this company?" You don't want to answer this question with something like, "Because this company has a job open in my field and I need a job." When they ask you this question, their expectation is to hear about what you know of the company and what about that information appeals to you. So make sure you're prepared to answer with that expectation in mind.

You may also want to do some research about the individual interviewer, if you know his or name ahead of time. The best way to find out professional information is to look up the individual on LinkedIn.com, or on the company's website. That way, you can ask the interviewer questions particular to his or her experience. However, you want to be sure to keep the questions professional. If you have questions about whether something would be appropriate, you might want to practice the questions with someone you trust.

Interviewing the Interviewer

Remember, even though the power is with the employer to offer you the job or not, the interview process is still mutual. Even if they offer you the job, you don't have to take it if you feel that the employer, company, or working environment would not be a good fit for you. It's in your best interest to ask effective questions in order to find out what it's like to work for the company, and in the group you would be joining. When you're planning potential responses to interview questions, try to think of some good questions to ask that will help you determine how the company, management, and department would be a fit for you.

In Our Own Words

I try to turn [an] interview around so I'm interviewing them. Why would I want to work for you? This gives me confidence . . . as well as keeps me from working somewhere where the environment is not comfortable. I've done that, never again. —Doug Sparling, Adult on the Autism Spectrum

You may think, "I need a job, why would I turn one down that is offered?" There are times when you won't have an option. But if you have some flexibility, think hard about whether the job is a good fit. You don't want to take a job that you will wind up quitting or being fired from in a short period of time. That won't look good on your resume, and the stress may adversely affect your health, which will make it even harder to be productive and may have serious repercussions for you, personally.

So what are the right questions to ask a potential employer? You should be sure to ask specific questions to determine the culture of the department and the management styles of the leadership:

- How would you describe what a typical day for someone in this role might look like?

- How do you prefer to work with your employees? Are you more "hands on" or "hands off"?

- Is this position new or existing? If it's an existing role, why did the previous employee leave? (If you ask this question, interviewers will rarely directly say, "He got fed up with us and quit." But, if an employee left for neutral reasons, like he moved away, or he got a great offer, but still has a good relationship with the managers, that's a good sign. If the interviewer is evasive and gives you a very brief but ambiguous answer, taken together with the answers to the other questions, this may be a warning sign about the management style or culture of the department.)

You will have to make the decision based on your own preferences, but my own experience has been that it's better to take a lesser job with a better culture than a great job with an awful one. For those of us who live with a high level of stress anyway, taking on additional stress will not help us to be successful in life. Insomuch as you can control it, stress in your life should come from fulfilling things—stretching yourself to try something new, or taking on a professional challenge that only you can do. Stress shouldn't come from dealing with a manager or coworkers who don't trust you, treat you with disrespect, or just don't adapt to your style in the same way you adapt to theirs. A good workplace should recognize how you work best, and support it, because they know that allowing you to work in such a way that enables you to be productive benefits the company. A company that doesn't do this is often not a good place to work for anyone, let alone someone on the spectrum.

Disclosure in the Interviewing Process

Disclosure is an issue that will impact every person on the spectrum in different ways. For some, the differences that autism brings are such that you will have to disclose, at least partially, in order to successfully navigate the interview. For example, if you will need an aide, or an AAC device during the interview, you will likely need to disclose. In that case, the challenge is in how to do so. For those who are able to partially or fully "pass" as neurotypical, disclosure can be a difficult decision. The question of when to disclose can also be a difficult one. Even though we have antidiscrimination laws, such as the Americans with Disabilities Act (ADA), laws don't always change behavior, and violations are difficult to prove.

This is especially true with discrimination that happens prior to being hired. Those that discriminate in the hiring process will rarely be open about their reasons. In some cases, they may not even be aware that they are discriminating. They may have a subconscious distrust of people who are different, or they may not want to admit to themselves that they are prejudiced. If they are open about it, they will likely only be open about it to people who have a loyalty to them, or who share their views. If that is the case, how can you prove that it is discrimination?

Even if you could, would you want to? If you sued the company, and forced them to submit any materials regarding your hire, or somehow got someone to testify on your behalf that the employer said that they were not hiring you because you have a disability, what would the outcome be? Would you want to work for a company that treated you that way? If you win, and just get some money, will it be worth it? Will other employers be afraid to hire you because they believe you might sue them, too? All of these are the considerations that people who are part of a minority group face, whether they are female, part of an ethnic or religious minority, or have some kind of disability.

The unfortunate fact is that many people don't truly understand what autism or Asperger's syndrome is, and what people don't understand, they often fear. What people do know is often connected with the many charities that emphasize the challenges of being on the spectrum in order to motivate people to donate to their charity. Unfortunately, that means, for many people, what comes to mind when you state the word "autism" is not competence or talent, but deficits and what we can't do. For an employer who doesn't know better, they might assume that hiring someone on the autism spectrum is charity, or that we simply wouldn't be able to do the job.

Please don't misunderstand what I am saying. Many on the spectrum do face extreme challenges, and that should not be ignored. However, the way many charities represent autism, mixed with our culture's very simplistic understanding of what disability is all about, can be devastating to many of us who are seeking deeper inclusion in the world. The reality is that I, you, and everyone else on the spectrum need to help the world understand that having challenges—even extreme ones—does not mean a person does not have abilities and contributions to make to the world. Ability isn't a binary thing. Unfortunately, many people who have limited experience with disabilities tend to act like it is, so when challenges are emphasized, lack of ability is assumed.

When you go in for an interview, you don't know whether the interviewer is one of these people. Is she the type of person who will make assumptions about your abilities based on hearing the label "autism" or "Asperger's" alone, or will she listen to you and assess your abilities based on actual knowledge about you? Whether you choose to call yourself autistic, a person with autism, a person with Asperger's, aspie, autie, Aspergian, or Aspergerian, the fact is that you want an interviewer to see *you*, not her stereotypes about your label.

If you already know this person, or have been referred to him by someone who confirms that he has an awareness of autism, you may feel more comfortable disclosing. In other cases, choosing to disclose is to gamble on the interviewer's awareness of autism, and/or his willingness not to prejudge. If you have the choice, you will need to decide whether you are comfortable with taking that chance. If the potential employer is an inclusive one, there may be some benefit to disclosure.

If one of the aspects of autism you face is auditory processing issues, then disclosure may make a phone interview easier to navigate. This way, you could request that you hold the interview via TTY, or via Skype or FaceTime, if you're able to compensate by reading lips. In this type of a situation, you may choose only to disclose your *needs*, but not your diagnosis.

What do I mean by this? Well, in the case of a phone interview, this could mean saying to the person scheduling the interview, "I don't hear well on the phone, could we conduct it by video via Skype or FaceTime? This will help me to understand, as I can read lips." In the case of having difficulties with verbal speech, it would mean saying, "I have a condition that impacts my ability to verbalize speech, so I use an AAC device." One script I have used is, "I have a condition that sometimes makes it difficult for me to process verbal speech, so sometimes I am slow in responding to a question. Could you please allow me a little extra time to process your question and formulate my answer? That would help me a lot, thank you."

If you do choose to use the term autism or Asperger's, try not to use the term in isolation. If you are dealing with someone who has little to no experience with autism, she will likely have a very simplistic and/or stereotyped view of it. She may be confused if you don't fit her preconception. To minimize this, always follow up with a statement of what having autism means in your case, specifically the aspects of it that you think may be relevant to that particular situation. You might say something like, "I have autism. This means that I have a difficult time making eye contact, and sometimes I stutter or am a little bit slower to speak than average. If you could please be patient with me, I'd really appreciate it."

Any time you disclose, whether you choose to just partially disclose according to your needs in the situation, or whether you choose to fully disclose, it always helps to end the statement with a request to the other person regarding how he can support you. This helps him to understand how you would like him to respond to the situation, and may reduce some of his anxiety, especially if he hasn't had experience with someone with that particular challenge before. Most people want to help but may not know the appropriate response. So make it easy for them and provide them the appropriate response. If it's a reasonable request, which is put politely, I have rarely experienced a situation where the person wouldn't respect it.

Once you have decided which strategy you want to take with regard to disclosure, you'll want to make sure that you take the time to script this out for yourself, so that you have a plan as to what you want to say. Try to come up with different variations based on the typical areas of challenges you might experience. For sensory overload, you might say, "I have a neurological condition that makes it hard to effectively process sensory input; the combination of noise and fluorescent lighting in this room will make it very difficult for me to concentrate. Could we conduct this interview in an alternate location?" If you are concerned that some may be put off by stimming that you can't control, then come up with something to say in that situation.

If you are able, there may be some situations in which you may consciously choose not to say anything about your diagnosis. This all depends on what you feel comfortable with, and how much you think that your behavioral or sensory differences will potentially impact the outcome of the interview if they aren't explained.

Planning What to Bring with You

When you're called for an interview, it's important to ask a few questions to make sure that you're prepared. You'll want to make sure you write down the date, time, and location of the interview, the name of the person who contacted you, the names of the people you will be interviewing with, the expected length of the interview, as well as who to contact if something occurs and you need to reschedule or cancel. It's also a good idea to ask the person who contacts you to describe the typical interview process to you, so that you know what to expect.

Will you be meeting with one person, or many? If more than one, will you interview with them as a group, or will you have separate interviews with each of them? Will you need to fill out an employment application prior to the interview, or take a skills test? Are there any specific items or pieces of information they recommend that you bring? Asking these questions will help you in the planning process.

There are some items you will always want to bring with you, such as hard copies of your cover letter and resume so that you can provide a replacement if the interviewers forget to bring their copy. When you get ready to go to the interview, make sure that you have enough printed copies of these items (on bond or resume paper) to be able to distribute one to each interviewer, keep one for your own reference during the interview, and try to have at least one or two copies extra, in case something happens and one gets damaged, ripped, or you find you're asked to interview with more people than you expected. You will be expected to be able to talk about the items on your resume, so be prepared!

It's often a good idea to bring something to write with and a pad of paper to take notes. If you don't take full notes, that's okay. Just jot down the things you feel are important in what an interviewer is saying. (Don't write anything that you don't want an interviewer to read. People aren't supposed to read over another person's shoulder, but people often do anyway.) If handwriting is difficult for you, you could skip this, but if you do, make sure that you do what you can to make sure that you are focused on the interview, and what the interviewer is saying. Bringing an iPad or computer to take notes (unless you need it for AAC) may be misunderstood by the interviewer, and may send the message that you're not paying attention to her.

You may be asked to fill out a job application prior to your interview. In some companies, an application is just a formality and gets very little attention, except to be filed away, but you will still need to be prepared. You will need to have available the addresses and names of prior employers, names of contacts and phone numbers at those companies, and you may have to answer questions such as, "Why did you leave this employer?" Try to be prepared for these questions prior to arriving at the interview. You may also need a full address of your high school and any colleges you may have attended. You'll also need to be able to provide names and contact information for at least three references. Some job applications will request your salary at each prior company.

Many career experts will recommend that you avoid providing salary information to the employer prior to receiving a job offer, especially if you have been underemployed (and/or underpaid) previously. If you provide this at the beginning, you may be limiting your capability for increasing your salary. Once an employer sees your previous salary they may negotiate from that number, instead of starting from a higher number within the salary range set for the position. If there is a large difference between what you made and the salary for the job, then they may question why you were paid so little, if you were such a great employee. If there are spaces for this on the application, recommendations vary, but some suggestions are to write NA or a dash in the box.

Avoid taking with you anything that would serve as a distraction in the interview. If you have a cell phone, turn the ringer off or leave it in the car. Be careful not to spill any food or drink on your clothing, and don't take any of it with you to the interview. (It's okay to have a candy bar or some other emergency food in your purse or bag, as long as it's securely closed and clearly out of sight. An interviewer should not be able to smell it, either.) The interviewer has set aside this time to interview you, and it is courteous to give your full attention to the interview as well. This is true even if the interviewer is not paying you full attention.

Some candidates will bring additional materials to the interview to supplement the resume and cover letter. One example is an interview presentation, which is a PowerPoint presentation that provides an overview of your skills and abilities in an easy to read, engaging way. These allow you to place emphasis on specific aspects of your traits, skills, and abilities about which you specifically want the employer to know. You may also want to bring a portfolio of examples representing your previous work. This is very helpful in fields where the product of your work is reproducible. (Be careful that you do not include any examples that include confidential information from a previous employer. However impressive the sample, breaking confidentiality will get you excluded from consideration very quickly.)

Ideally, you want any of these additional items to be copies of your originals. As great as they are, the interviewer may not remember them unless she can refer to them later. She may want to take this information back and show it to her manager, or other members of the team. One good way to do this might be to create a website that you reference on your resume that prospective employers can review whenever they like. You want to make it easy for them to persuade others that you are a good hire, so make sure you bring enough copies of these types of materials for all interviewers, just like you did with your resumes.

Planning What You Will Wear

When you are preparing for your interview, make sure you plan what you will wear. Make sure that the clothes are clean and in good repair. Going to an interview in pants with frayed ends or shirts with rips in them will not send a good impression. If the clothes require ironing, make sure that you do so. All of your clothing should be neat and clean (as should you).

What you wear will depend on the type of job you're applying for, and the dress code of the company (the rules about what clothes are considered appropriate in that company's culture). If you're not sure what that is, you can ask the person scheduling the interview what the office's dress code is. If you don't get that opportunity, then you're better off choosing more conservative attire. For men, this means a suit and tie, with dress shoes and dark socks. For women, it means a conservative dress or suit, panty hose, and heels. This may prove difficult for you if these types of clothes cause problems with your sensory sensitivities. Unfortunately, these comprise the typical "uniform" for an interview, and you may be judged negatively for not dressing appropriately.

If you are able to find out the company's dress code, then you would typically want to dress at least as nicely as their regular employees, but if at all possible, you want to dress nicer. The typical kinds of dress codes include the following:

- Business/business formal—typically a suit and tie for men with dark socks and black dress shoes; and a conservative dress or women's suit for women, panty hose, and heels or dress flats.

- Business casual—typically a button-down shirt and khaki dress pants with loafers or oxfords, and dress socks (shoes and socks don't have to be black; they can be brown) for men; for women, a casual career-type dress and flats or a button-down shirt, dress pants/khakis, and career casual shoes.

- Casual/jeans casual—both men and women are allowed to wear jeans. Polo shirts are usually okay. T-shirts with logos, skimpy tank tops, flip flops, or tennis shoes are usually not allowed. Shoes and socks are often similar to business casual.

Based on what you learn of a company's dress code, move one bullet up, and that is the *minimum* form of dress that you want to appear in. It never hurts you to dress more formally, however. If you show up dressed very formally, very clean and very neat, many employers will take that as a sign that you really want the job, that you put that amount of effort into your appearance. You can never go wrong with dressing business formal.

For men, if you are not sure about how to choose a suit, you can either ask for someone experienced to help you, or go to a place that specializes in suits and tell them what you need the suit for, and they can help you choose something appropriate. These places will often tailor a suit to fit you, which may help minimize the sensory issues. You may also want to try a variety of shirts and ties to see which ones feel least uncomfortable to you. If you note a certain type of fabric or weave works best for you, make a note of this for the future.

For women, if you're not sure what dresses might be appropriate for business formal or business casual, you can ask an experienced friend or family member to come along with you to pick one out. It may also help to review pictures on retailers' websites. Many of them will categorize dresses by function. They will call them "work" or "career casual." However, don't confuse the term "formal" as used on these websites with the "formal" in business formal. In the context of the listings on the websites, "formal" means the types of dresses you'd wear to a banquet or ball. They are the equivalent of a tuxedo for men. They are way too dressy and/or flashy for work, and often show way too much skin for a professional environment. "Cocktail" dresses are also generally not appropriate for wearing to work.

Overall, for any interview, you're best wearing dark colors like black or navy. If you wear jewelry of any kind, it should be minimal and conservative. (Small earring studs, a small gold ring, and/or a small necklace would be appropriate.) Many employers will not like nose or lip piercings, so you will likely want to take them out for the interview. Also, many employers don't like visible tattoos, so if you have one that is visible, it's a good idea to cover it up. Avoid perfume or cologne, or use it very sparingly. You don't want the interviewer to be distracted from what you're saying by an overwhelming scent.

Tips for a Good Interview

The best thing that you can do to ensure a good interview is to prepare well. I'd also recommend learning as much as you can about the process. What I've included here can't possibly cover all different interview formats you'll encounter, or the full range of the types of questions you might ask or be asked. To learn more, I highly recommend a book called *Active Interviewing: Branding, Selling, and Presenting Yourself to Win Your Next Job* by Eric P. Kramer.

This book covers interviewing in depth, providing scripted answers to tough questions, such as questions about compensation and why you might have left a previous job. It also covers how to create an interview presentation (and provides examples), gives specific guidance on the type of body language to display during an interview, and what you can do prior to an interview to increase your confidence. In addition, it has some excellent suggestions regarding how to handle postinterview follow-up.

Other places you can get advice on interviewing are at the job sites I mentioned in the previous chapter. In addition to job listings, most of these sites have newsletters and many quality articles on every aspect of job searching, including interviews. The About.com Job Searching (*http://jobsearch.about.com*) website is an incredibly comprehensive resource covering everything from planning your job search to interviewing to negotiating salary. Make sure you specifically spend some time learning about salary negotiation.

If you prefer classes or presentations, download iTunes and search iTunes U, where you can access free talks and materials from some of the top universities in the world. There are many

classes available on iTunes U about interviewing and job searching. Many libraries also have classes for job hunters that can provide guidance on interviewing. In addition, there's an e-learning
site called LatitudeU (*www.latitudeU.com*) that has many different
e-learning courses on interviewing and job searching, many of
which are free.

If you need to see examples of appropriate interview body
language, search "interview body language" on YouTube. There
are good videos on this subject by About.com, and by BNET.com,
made available on its BNETvideo YouTube channel. The BNET
video, entitled "How to Ace a Job Interview," is narrated by Carol
Kinsey Goman, PhD, author of *The Nonverbal Advantage: Secrets
and Science of Body Language at Work*. If you're looking to understand nonverbal body language in the workplace better, this book
may also be worthwhile to read.

The Day of Your Interview

When it comes time for your interview, you want to feel as at ease
as possible. If meditation or deep breathing helps you, take a few
quiet minutes to do this in a private place, like your car or a bathroom stall. Have a practiced greeting for both the interviewer and
for whoever is going to meet you, if it is not the interviewer himself.
Always be kind and polite to the front desk clerk or receptionist (you
never know what the interviewer will ask them about you later).

If you're unfamiliar with the route to the interview location,
you may want to take a trial run to the interview location in the
days prior to the interview. Pay attention to how long it takes.
Because commute times can vary so much based on time and
day, try to do it at a similar day and time to when the interview
will be held. When you plan your route to the interview, take the

time it took you to travel to the location and multiply it by 1.5 (You want to have extra time in case a bus is late or you run into traffic. If the route is particularly busy, you may want to up this to 2 or 2.5), add twenty minutes (you would like to arrive fifteen totwenty minutes early), add the amount of time it will take you to get ready (make sure you account for the additional time it will take you to dress in interview clothes, do your hair neatly, etc.), then add another twenty minutes (in case something goes wrong while you're getting ready).

After you've added up all of this time, subtract this amount from the interview time, and this will tell you when you need to get up or start preparing for the interview. There is a lot of padding in this number, so you may find that you're there very early. If so, simply wait outside the building, or in the lobby, until fifteen or twenty minutes prior to the interview. It's better to be early than being late because you spilled coffee on your shirt, smeared your mascara, or misplaced your glasses.

In addition, you want to take extra care with your hygiene prior to an interview. You want to be freshly showered, and with your hair styled (a suit will do no good if you show up with your hair flat and wet). Wear deodorant. Make sure your teeth are well brushed and you don't have bad breath. You might want to suck on a breath mint while you travel to the interview, provided you can finish it prior to the interview time. Do not chew gum, or if you do, dispose of the gum prior to entering the building for the interview. You don't want the interviewer to be distracted or put off by bad breath, body odor, or the sight and sound of you smacking and chewing gum. Don't put on too much makeup, either.

From the time you enter the building, stand up tall, with your head up and shoulders back. Staring at the floor will not project a confident image. Go up to the front desk, or receptionist, tell him who you are, that you're there for an interview, what time the interview is for, and whom it is with. The receptionist will usually notify the interviewer that you are there. He may give you an employment application to fill out while you wait. If he doesn't tell you what to do with it after you've completed it, then ask. Some companies ask you to keep it until you're sent in for the interview, and then give it to the interviewer. Other times, you will be asked to return it to the front desk or receptionist.

If you have to wait for a while for the interviewer to come, try to stay engaged and aware of what's going on around you. Don't take out your phone and play games on it, or doodle on the pad of paper you've brought. You want to be alert and prepared when the interviewer comes out to meet you (sometimes, they won't come to get you, but the receptionist will show you to the room where the interview will occur). If the interviewer does come out to meet you personally, be prepared to greet her warmly. If you've done some investigating of her on LinkedIn or similar professional sites, and have seen her picture, you may recognize her from the picture. Otherwise, look for someone who appears to be looking around, wait a couple of minutes, then ask if she is the interviewer, or just listen for her to call your name.

The interviewer may approach you and say something like, "Are you Adam? I'm Roy Barnes. Nice to you meet you." At this point, you should already be in the process of extending your hand for the handshake. You can answer, "Yes, I am. Great to meet you!" Then give him a firm (but not painfully firm) handshake. Sometimes, the interviewer won't offer his name right away. If he simply asks, "Are you Adam?" you can respond, "Yes, I am. You must be Mr. Barnes. Great to meet you!" Once again, follow up with a handshake. If this exchange took place in the lobby, then the interviewer will likely show you to the interviewing location. Otherwise, the interview will begin.

Each interview will be different, because each interviewer is different and has a different interviewing style. Some will just ask the standard questions. Others may offer you a problem, or a hypothetical scenario, and ask you how you would respond. Hopefully, you will have anticipated that question, or at least one that is similar. Assuming you're interviewing in a field that you are passionate about, if they provide you a typical problem you'd face on the job and ask how you would resolve it, that's a great time to show your expertise. Just do what you would do if you were on the job. Some employers may actually ask you to complete a sample task. This is also helpful for those of us on the spectrum, because it allows us to show our capabilities rather than just talk about them.

Here are a few tips to follow during an interview:

- Don't swear. Even if the interviewer uses this type of language, don't join in.

- Smile frequently. This projects warmth and engagement (even if the other person isn't smiling back).

- When the interviewer is talking, send signals that you are listening. Do this by nodding your head periodically, while occasionally saying, "Mmm, hmm." Make eye contact, if possible.

- Don't forget to ask questions! Have a few follow-up questions prepared for the end of the interview. If they finish the interview by asking if you have any questions, being able to ask a few shows interest in the job.

- Try to answer all questions in a positive manner. For example, if you're asked, "Why are you leaving your job?" and the truth is because you hate your boss, don't say that. Instead, focus on what you *do* want. "I'm looking to work for a company where

I can receive the support I need, where I can grow and learn new things."

- At the end of the interview, shake hands with the interviewer, say that it was nice to meet him, and thank him or her politely for his time.

- Often, an interviewer will give you her business card and invite you to contact her if you have any questions. Make sure you keep track of her card if she does; you'll need it for post-interview follow up, which we will cover in the next section. It is a good idea to keep the interview notes together with a business card (or the information gathered) from the interviewer and file these in case she doesn't call back for some time.

Handling Compensation Questions

Don't rush to ask questions about compensation or benefits. The majority of the first interview should be dedicated to simply getting to know your interviewer, learning about the company and the job, and assessing how you feel you would fit into it. Let the interviewer bring up the subject of compensation, but be prepared. Make sure you know what number you hope for, even if you don't share it. You can look up common salary ranges at *www.bls.gov*, or on sites like *http://salary.com*. If you are pressed to provide salary expectations, try to get the interviewer to give you a salary range first, so that you can see where your number lands in regard to that range.

In response to these questions, you can say, "Well, I am interested to know what the salary range for this job is." The amount of compensation you previously received is not necessarily relevant to the present situation and doesn't in any way put you in a good negotiating position to reveal it. If you made much more in a previous position and want the current job, even though it is a downgrade in salary, the interviewer could decide that you may accept a lower paying job and stay just until you find one that pays closer to what you received in your previous job, when, in fact, that might not be true at all.

If the previous job paid less, the interviewer may utilize that information to decide to offer you less, or, that for some reason you are not qualified to earn the current salary—again, even if this is an inaccurate assumption. If you absolutely have to, then state a salary range ("I'd like to make between $60,000 and $70,000 a year.") Understand that if your range matches the employer's range and you are given an offer, the employer will most likely choose a number right between the two numbers you give. Try to choose your range accordingly.

Post Interview

Making it through the interview is tough, but sometimes the waiting afterwards is harder. In the meantime, it's polite to write the interviewer a thank-you note. In the context of a job interview, a thank-you note is different than a thank-you note you'd send to a friend, for example. Similar to a cover letter, your thank-you note will both thank the interviewer for her time but also reinforce the topics you spoke about in the interview that you want to emphasize. A follow-up e-mail (sent the same or next day) is also very acceptable and will get recognition sooner. For examples, see the books and resources mentioned previously.

After the interview, most often you can expect one of four major outcomes:

- You are contacted, and the company makes you a job offer.

- They contact you for a follow-up interview with a different interviewer(s).

- You receive a call or a letter indicating another candidate was chosen for the position.

- You don't receive any communication from the company regarding the job.

If you are made an offer, then the negotiation process begins. While there are a lot of aspects to the salary negotiation process, it would be difficult to cover them all here. But begin with the knowledge that you don't have to accept the first offer you're given. In fact, most people don't. Some employers may even think less of you if you do accept the first offer, as this can make it look like you don't have confidence in your worth. Even if the salary they offer you is higher than you had hoped to make, that may simply mean that you undervalued yourself. It's worth it to make at least one attempt to get them to increase your offer.

Once you receive the offer, assess it against what you were hoping for. Is it very low? A little low? About right? Based on this assessment, reference various career resources I've provided so far to determine your best strategy for negotiation, or ask someone whom you trust, and whom you know is good at negotiation, to advise you. Keep in mind that in many organizations, you can also negotiate some things that would be considered benefits, like paid vacation time.

If you are contacted for a follow-up interview, the process will be similar to the first. The fact that they are contacting you for a follow-up interview is a good sign. It means that your performance on the first interview was good enough that they want you to come back. There are a many reasons that they might do this. One reason is that many companies use a multiple-step recruiting process. You may meet with a lower-level person, and then if that person likes you, you need to meet other members of the team, or even management. Another reason is that there may be an opening in the company that you don't know about, and the first interviewer thinks you would be a good fit for that position, which reports to someone else. Either way, be encouraged. They're interested!

If an employer contacts you to tell you that you didn't get the job, don't get discouraged. It happens to everyone. One thing you might want to do, however, is to write a follow-up letter to the rejection. Many job search books recommend this. You respond to the rejection letter and thank the interviewer for his response, reiterate your interest in the position, and ask him to keep you in mind if the job should open up again. This keeps the interviewer thinking of you, and if by some chance the person chosen doesn't work out, he may call you up and ask you if you're interested.

Finally, if you don't hear anything back from the employer, don't be surprised, and don't take it personally. Nowadays, this is fairly typical. In many organizations, the only candidate who will be told the status of the job is the one who got the job. While this is not very nice to the other interviewees, it's not uncommon. Although it's natural to feel anxious, don't give into the temptation to call the interviewer or pester her to tell you the status of your application. This won't endear you to her, and may make the company less likely to hire you in the future. Instead, simply recognize that this is one you didn't get, and move on to the next one. If they change their mind, they'll call you.

Remember, although the most common cause of not hearing back is not getting the job, it could also be that the company put in place a "hiring freeze" so that no managers could hire anyone, or it could be that other circumstances delayed their filling the job. It could be that they hired someone, but that person won't work out, and they may call you in the future. Try not to worry about it. No one ever gets every job he applies for, and that's okay.

POINTS TO REMEMBER

- The purpose of an interview is to help you and the prospective employer to assess if you will be a good fit for the job.

- Before the interview, prepare and memorize scripted responses to the most common interview questions.

- Research the company and learn about your interviewer (but don't invade her privacy!).

- It's a good idea to prepare a portfolio of work and/or an interview presentation to leave with the interviewer.

- At the interview, dress well, practice good etiquette, and be on time.

CHAPTER 9

Navigating the Workplace

Work. Ideally, it's about significance. It's about feeling that you're a part of the world, and that you have something to contribute. Receiving money for your contributions certainly helps as well. But for many of us on the autism spectrum, there are a lot of aspects of the typical workplace that can cause difficulties in achieving a sense of significance and meaningful contributions. In this chapter, we'll cover some of the kinds of challenges you may encounter, and give some recommendations as to how to overcome them. We'll cover things such as the unwritten rules of the workplace, body language, and office politics. We'll also discuss some of the ways in which you can use technology or make adaptations to minimize some of the challenges. In addition, we'll go over some ideas about how to find opportunities to utilize your strengths, and how to find supportive friends and mentors in the workplace.

The social environment of the workplace can be very confusing and complex, just as many other social situations are. I will not be able to cover every possible situation you may encounter, but I will try to cover some basics. Early in this book, I recommended reading *Emily Post's Etiquette: Manners for a New World* as a reference for learning about communication and the social world in general. As a basic reference, it's a good book. I also recommend reading the counterpart to this book, catered specifically for the workplace, called *Emily Post's The Etiquette Advantage in Business: Personal Skills for Professional Success, Second Edition*. This will give you a good start at understanding the correct rules to follow in the workplace.

When I think about etiquette, I find it's easier for me to think about it in terms of what it's meant to do. Etiquette rules usually are practiced to show respect for others. The reasons behind them are not always explained, but if you ask, or think about it, there's usually a reason behind each rule that makes sense. You just have to figure out what that purpose is. If you find that purpose, it makes etiquette seem less like a list of random rules, and makes them easier to remember. Sometimes, the purpose for one rule will suggest other rules that are good to follow.

Grooming

When I was in school, I remember a conversation that occurred during a parent's night at the school. One of the adults said that a teacher looked like "an unmade bed." I was confused. He didn't look at all like a bed to me. He looked like a human being. Why would someone say he looked like a bed? Eventually, I figured out (or somebody told me) that he was referring to the state of his clothing. He was wearing a button-down shirt and a jacket, but they were very wrinkled and his jacket wasn't on right.

I hadn't noticed. It was clear that they felt that "looking like an unmade bed" was something that was not desirable, but why that should be escaped me. He was a teacher. His job was to convey information to us in such a way that we could understand it. What did wrinkles in his shirt and a jacket with a lapel flipped backward have to do with anything? I was tempted to wonder—did they think somehow that wrinkles removed knowledge of how to teach from his brain?

This is one of the ways that rules around grooming can be confusing. It can seem illogical that grooming should be an issue in this type of situation. Back then, I was thinking about it in terms of his intrinsic abilities. It was demonstrably false to me that wrinkles in a shirt would have any relationship to intellectual abilities. However, since then, I've come to learn that the people who made the comments weren't thinking about it that way. Not knowing him, they were looking for clues as to what sort of person he was.

In order to teach, you need to have the organizational skills to effectively manage the administrative tasks related to teaching. If he couldn't organize himself well enough to iron his shirt, check how his hair looked, or ensure his jacket was on straight prior to meeting a group of parents, then what must his administrative skills be like? If he didn't *lack* organizational skills (which might impact his teaching), then it must mean that he didn't *care* enough to make the effort to look neat. If he didn't care, what did that say about his commitment to his teaching job?

Secondarily, as a teacher, he was a person in a position of authority, and he needed to communicate that to his students. If you think about the most common representations of authority, like a general in the military, a policeman, CEO, or president, what do they look like? They usually appear very neat. Because appearing neat is associated with authority in the minds of most people, when they saw him looking the way he did, a second assumption was made. He didn't *look* like their idea of authority, so they questioned his effectiveness in running the classroom authoritatively.

Embedded in these judgments are some assumptions that are faulty, many of which could impact those of us on the spectrum disparately. For example, putting on clothes can be a challenging motor task. If a person is clumsy, he may not feel comfortable using an iron because he is afraid of burning himself or the garment. The unfortunate fact of the matter is that people who don't have experiences with conditions like autism often don't even think about these types of challenges. I saw this in how my teacher was treated. He had a harder time than the other teachers.

This is an example of one way grooming can become a problem—one which you can avoid by adhering to certain rules. You follow these rules to prevent others from making unfair character judgments about you. The need to do this may seem unfair, but I believe it's a symptom of how the social world developed. In our early times, a human's ability to survive rested on being able to quickly assess danger through external appearance alone. To this day, human beings are still doing it.

Survival and danger are now defined somewhat differently. Nowadays, humans use these methods to assess whether the person will be a bad employee, will effectively lead your company, or will be unreliable and cause you emotional hurt or monetary damages, etc. These tendencies were amplified in my teacher's case, because human beings in general are very protective of their kids. Any indication that a person in a position to supervise, teach, or assist their kids may not be reliable or up to the task is sure to trigger an instinctual concern and protectiveness of their young. Thus my teacher's challenges.

This is why your choices in clothing, hair style, and jewelry are considerations in the workplace. Regardless of the nature of your job, and how your skills fit that job, these social drives among fellow humans will often interfere with their perception of your fitness for the job if you do not appear "professional." From your perspective, you may have chosen to wear a soft T-shirt, not because you don't care about your job, but because other shirts cause sensory issues. Most people will not automatically come to that conclusion.

You will have to decide what your strategy will be for handling instances where the requirements (written or unwritten) of the job environment dictate that you wear clothes that are uncomfortable for you. While you may be able to disclose the difficulties your sensory issues create to your manager or other employees, you may still face judgment from other people in the company who don't know you personally.

Most companies have printed guidelines as to how to dress appropriately, and when you are a new hire, you should receive a copy of these guidelines (if not, it's a good idea to ask for one). Take a look at these guidelines and see if any of the listed options will work for you, and if there are any that absolutely won't work. Many times, when an HR person describes (or even in an online article) what a particular dress code typically is, she will give you a very simplistic list of what that means.

Try to work with family, friends, or someone you trust to come up with alternatives that fit these guidelines but that cause you less sensory discomfort. Maybe you can go to a store where you can try on some different options. For example, if cotton button-down shirts are uncomfortable for you, what about silk or a softer kind of fabric? It may be slightly more expensive (and it may be slightly different from what management expects), but it may be close enough to still be considered in compliance with the dress code.

When you're not able to come up with workable alternatives, try to come up with some options that you can tolerate that are as close to the options provided as possible. When you approach your boss about the issue, you then have an alternative you can offer. You might say, "I have a condition that makes ties very uncomfortable to wear. Would it be okay if I wore a dressy sweater vest under my jacket instead?" Also, watch to see how much employees vary from the dress code as it is written. You may be able to pick up on patterns as to which items are more readily enforced than others. You may note that in a business casual environment, you almost never see jeans, but sometimes you do see sandals. Or you may observe that while the official dress code mandates panty hose, most women don't wear them.

This gives you an idea of which aspects of the dress code your boss may be more willing to be flexible about, versus those that are hard and fast rules. If your dress code requires pantyhose if you wear dresses or skirts, that rule may be overlooked if you choose to wear shin- or ankle-length dresses. People rarely look at your ankles to see if you have pantyhose on (unless you have *very* hairy legs, which is why shaving or depilatories are important). If you really needed to wear some type of hosiery, they won't be able to tell a difference between knee highs or pantyhose, as long as the upper band on the knee highs are strong enough to keep them up. You may also try to see if tights work better for you than panty-hose. They might look a little bit different, but they accomplish the same task (covering up your legs).

Overall, unless you work in a very formal or rigid environment, as long as you can dress fairly close to the dress code, your clothes are in good repair, and your clothes and hair are neat, you're usually okay. However, there a few more considerations that you absolutely need to consider.

Undergarments

Whatever your gender, it's important to make sure that your underpants aren't visible in any outfit you are wearing. This style is sometimes tolerated in schools, but when it comes to a professional environment, it's not. In most environments, women should wear a bra. If you don't wear a bra, people can often tell either by how your breasts move under your shirt, or because they can see the outline of your nipples. This can be distracting, and may be misinterpreted by some as an attempt to be sexually provocative.

If seams or underwire bras are difficult for you to tolerate, sports bras may be an option, as might certain types of seamless bras, such as certain bras marketed under the names Ahh Bra or Genie Bra. Making sure you choose the right size will also minimize discomfort. The wrong size not only makes the bras tight, uncomfortable, and pinching, but it can affect the appearance of your clothes in a negative way, or make you appear provocative. You don't want to wear a bra that is so tight that sensitive parts of you pop out of it at the wrong times. If you're not sure of the correct size to purchase, go to a retailer where they have people who will measure you to ensure you get the right size.

If the straps bother you, and strapless bras are too tight, you might consider wearing a strapless corset or bustier. These more old-fashioned undergarments sometimes work because they distribute deep pressure more evenly across your body. For some, it may even serve a similar purpose to weighted vests used by some on the spectrum. It really depends on how your neurology responds. Choose one that covers your breasts adequately, and that has a color and construction that will not be too obvious under your typical clothes. If it's visible underneath your clothing, it may provoke a similar reaction to going without a bra, as these garments are considered by some to be sexually provocative (think about early outfits Madonna wore). So choose your combination of clothes and undergarments accordingly.

Avoid Dressing Provocatively

What does "dressing provocatively" mean? Dressing provocatively, in general, means dressing in a way that will provoke sexual interest in you. This means any outfit that shows a lot of skin, especially outfits that show a lot of your chest, back, or legs. It may mean a blouse that reveals a lot of your chest, or it may mean wearing extremely short skirts or shorts that show a lot of your legs. Most dress codes are specifically worded to prevent such outfits in the workplace, so if you stay as close to the dress code as possible, you will likely avoid most mistakes in this regard.

You may find, though, that your reactions to certain sensory issues may predispose you to inadvertently dress provocatively. For example, if you can't stand any fabric against your neck, you may be tempted to wear your shirts unbuttoned or buy low-cut tops. It's best for you if you can find a way to accommodate your sensory issues some other way, as dressing provocatively is considered very inappropriate in the workplace. Dressing this way is seen as a distraction from the matter at hand (the work).

Makeup

In many work environments, it's usually not a bad idea for women to wear makeup, although not all women do. If you do, try to wear very light makeup. You might apply some concealer to minimize dark circles under your eyes, a little eye shadow in neutral shades, and/or some mascara and subtle eyeliner. You can also wear neutral lipstick or lip gloss. If you wear blush, wear only a little; you don't want to look like you have a fever. If you have a fairly even skin tone, you probably don't need to wear foundation, but if you have blotchy skin or blemishes, you might want to consider it. If you have problems with liquid foundation, like I did for many years, you can try some of the new mineral makeups available on the market. Originally, these products were very expensive, but you can now find cheaper versions in drug stores.

If you like beauty and read a lot of beauty magazines, you're best off saving your makeup experiments for evenings and weekends. It can be fun to play with makeup to try to look like the models in the pictures, but the types of makeup styles used in the fashion industry are not typically appropriate for any workplace, except one that's a part of the fashion industry itself. Dark, thick, or vibrantly colored eye makeup is typically not appropriate, nor is applying glitter or rhinestones to the skin or face. If you wear this kind of makeup after hours, make sure you wash it off completely before going to work. You don't want to show up at work with black smudges underneath your eyes that make you look as if you've been punched.

If you are a male who typically wears makeup, check your company's dress policy to see if there are any rules on the subject. If there are, and you want to challenge it, discuss it with your boss or HR. As you decide whether to do so, be aware that some people hold strong biases against gender expression, and their judgments may impact you negatively. You'll want to plan your actions accordingly.

Hair

Most companies' dress codes will address the issue of appropriate hairstyles. At minimum, make sure that your hair is well brushed and neatly styled. Just as with makeup, you don't want to try hairstyles that are too elaborate or out of the mainstream when it comes to the office. Company policies vary when it comes to atypical hairstyles, such as Mohawks, or long hair for men. In many workplaces, such hairstyles are okay as long as they are kept neat and if hair that is long is brushed and pulled back in a ponytail. It usually is not okay to have a Mohawk styled so that it is sticking up. If the employer is particularly inflexible, then you may need to consider cutting your hair or wearing a different style. In most instances beards and mustaches should be well trimmed. If it is against your religion to cut your hair or trim your beard, you may need to request a religious accommodation via your company's HR department.

Basic Hygiene

Basic hygiene is important in general, and especially so in the workplace. First of all, most basic hygiene performs a health-related function. If you don't shower regularly, you may develop boils, or skin infections. If you don't brush your teeth on a regular basis (the American Dental Association recommends twice a day), you will develop bad breath, probably cavities (which will result in very uncomfortable dental work), and you may develop gum disease. All of these things can create real health concerns.

A more social reason to be concerned is that, if you don't do these things, it can make it unpleasant to be around you. If you do not shower or wash your hair often enough, you will eventually begin to have a foul body odor that may be detectable by others long before it is apparent to you (you may even become used to it and tune it out). If you don't brush your teeth, your breath will smell very bad, and some people may be disgusted by seeing the white plaque buildup in between and on your teeth. If you are sensitive to strong smells, such as perfumes or certain food cooking, recognize that the types of odors and sights caused by poor hygiene will cause the same type of distress to others as those things cause you.

Regularly bathing, washing your hair, and brushing your teeth are basic requirements in most workplaces, and there really isn't a way around that unless you work someplace completely alone, with no human contact. If you have difficulties in these areas, you will need to come up with some ways to stay clean that impact your sensory system the least, or try gradually desensitizing yourself by building up a tolerance to the sensations you find unpleasant. On the other hand, if you have challenges with executive skills that make it difficult to for you to sequence tasks, or to remember these tasks, try putting together visual schedules or checklists, or use one of the many mobile apps available to provide prompts and build schedules. PEAT, which I described earlier in the book, was designed specifically to help with tasks such as this.

The Niceties

Depending on the nature of your work, different levels of social interactions will be necessary. In almost every workplace, however, you'll be expected to respect what is commonly called "the niceties." Mostly, "the niceties" can be broken down into two categories: indications of courtesy and respect, and indications that you are thinking of others. Some cover both. Indications of courtesy and respect are things like smiling, saying "Hi!" or "Good morning!" to your coworkers, and thanking them when they've done something nice for you. Indications that you are thinking of others are things like noticing when someone is struggling with a heavy load and helping out by opening the door, or holding a door open for someone coming through a door behind you so that she is not smacked by it.

Indications of courtesy and respect may be less intuitive, because they represent preferences you may not share. The good thing about these is that they are codified very specifically in books like *Emily Post's Etiquette: Manners for a New World.* Overall, the purpose of these niceties is to acknowledge and show interest in other people as human beings, and to let them know that they're important enough to you that you notice them long enough to say, "Hi," or even "How are you?"

If you do not follow these typical rules, people will think you are rude, self-important (that you can't be bothered with them), arrogant, or stuck-up. Depending on the culture of your company/ department, however, you may find that you are forgiven for some of these, if you simply acknowledge to coworkers that you understand they are expected, that you didn't do them, apologize, and give a valid reason for not doing so. In today's busy workplace, workload often means there isn't much time to stop and chit chat. Often saying "Hi!" quickly to coworkers in the hall, then having a self-initiated ten to fifteen minute conversation about how they are is enough for them to recognize that you care.

For me, figuring out what the "thinking of others" items are is a little more intuitive (although, they, too, are usually covered by Emily Post). You can usually get pretty close to figuring out what these are by asking yourself what you would want if you were in the other persons' situation. How would you feel if you were in one of the following situations:

- You had a point you felt was really important, but someone was talking for a really long time, and you weren't given the opportunity to state your opinion.

- You were carrying a big load of boxes down a long hallway, and you were struggling to open a door, but were having a hard time doing so. You were afraid you might drop one of the boxes (which had something fragile in it). Someone approaches the door in the other direction.

- You were running really late to work, or for a meeting, and the door to the elevator you need to ride to the floor where your desk is located is about to close.

- You need to go to the bathroom and the toilet seat is all wet with someone else's pee.

- You want to make your lunch, but when you go to the lunch room to warm up your lunch, you find a pool of smelly fish soup in the microwave that you need to clean up.

In the first situation, would you feel frustrated? Would you wish that the person you were talking with would notice you have something to say and give you a moment to say it? Turn that around, and pretend that you're the one talking for a long time. Might someone feel the same? This is why it's one of "the niceties"—it shows that you care about the person and her feelings, if you take the moment to notice that she wants to talk, and then allow her to do so.

In the fourth scenario, how would you feel if you didn't see the moisture on the seat before you sat on it? Or if you did see it, how would you feel having to wipe up after someone else? Considering those feelings, what would you wish the person before you had done before leaving the bathroom? Apply this process to the rest of these scenarios.

What would you feel? What would you wish the other person had done to change the situation? What you wish he would do is often what you should do without being asked, if the situation were reversed. These are rules that many people in this culture now ignore, but they are rules that help others to see you as a caring and courteous person. The overall message you want to send to others through your actions is that you care about them, that you do for them what you would want others to do for you. Most people will reciprocate, if they see you do these things consistently.

"The niceties" also extend to attitudes about others. Do you like it when others speak badly about you, or make fun of the things you're not good at? Then it's a good idea not to do those things to others. Do you like it when your schedule is thrown off because someone is late? Then do what you can not to be late, and prevent causing issues like that yourself. If you think about it, many of the basic rules of etiquette (office or otherwise) track back to this concept. It's polite to do what you say that you will do, because if others make plans based on that commitment, it will adversely impact them.

It's expected for you to be punctual to meetings, and to your workday in general, because people have planned their day according to those meetings, and your manager has planned on your being at work at specific times (or at least for a reasonable amount of hours) so that you can get the tasks done he or she has assigned to you. If you don't manage your schedule appropriately, by being on time, or by allocating the appropriate amount of time to the list of duties you've been assigned in order to complete them within an appropriate timeline, this impacts your manager. This is also why it's polite to let others know if it appears you are going to be late to a scheduled meeting or event, so that they can plan accordingly.

Body Language

I won't go into great detail when it comes to body language, as we have already covered much of the relevant techniques in previous chapters, but I will cover a few items that relate specifically to the workplace. One item is commonly used types of body language. In the section on safety, we talked about dominant and submissive body language. It can be very helpful in the workplace to become familiar with these two categories of body language, both representing it and reading it, to some extent.

I know that some will have more issues with this than others. Personally, I have found that I am able to replicate some body language, and read some of it analytically, although it took a lot of study and work. Now, I often approach learning about body language like an investigation, as if I am an interpersonal Sherlock Holmes. I've found this analytical approach very useful. Interestingly enough, because I don't have the typical intuitive understanding of these things, there are times when intellectually analyzing body language can be *more* accurate than is the intuitive sense of those with a neurotypical makeup around me, precisely because I do it consciously and don't assume my "gut reaction" is right. It's a useful skill to be able to present dominant body language when you need to in order to be listened to. It can be helpful also to be able to see who is dominant in a group, and who is not. Sometimes the answer to that may surprise you. It may not be the most senior person in the room.

It's also useful to be able to identify when someone is treating you with respect or not. Indications of disrespect often are things like the following: A person doesn't look at you while speaking, leans away from you, or does other things while he is speaking. Indications of respect are things like the following: A person looks at you while you are speaking, remains quiet but nods or murmurs periodically to let you know she is listening, and asks you good questions. If you see signs of disrespect, it may be time to display some dominant body language. I'd suggest reading up on some of these indications, for the reasons mentioned here, in addition to the reasons given in the safety section.

Communication

Like body language, much of what we've discussed in previous chapters regarding communication applies directly to the employment world, so I won't restate most of it here. But I will go over a few important aspects of communication that apply directly to the workplace: conflict, diplomacy, and clarity.

Conflict

Conflict is common in the workplace and can be a significant source of stress. You will be able to minimize a lot of stress if you learn some conflict resolution and assertiveness skills. If you want to move up in a professional environment, these skills are things that you will be measured on, and they will be pivotal to your moving to a next step. A manager does not want to be called into every employee disagreement, This may make her feel like a parent to a bunch of little kids. There are a few basic things that have helped me to effectively deal with conflict.

First, if someone does something that offends you, don't assume that it is done so intentionally. Always ask. For example, a coworker says something offensive to you about a behavior connected to autism that he didn't know you have (or didn't know could be connected to autism). You get angry about it, inform him of such, and then step away to get calm. Once you're calm, you carefully draft an e-mail to the employee involved, explaining in reasonable terms why what he said was offensive.

You carefully break down what exactly he said that offended you, and why, and you provide a description of what your disability means for you and links to reputable sources describing it as well. You choose to give the coworker a chance to respond to the incident himself, prior to escalating it to the boss. The person involved reads the e-mail, but says nothing for the rest of the day.

The following morning, you come in to find an e-mail from your boss that says, "It appears there was an incident. Let's talk." Beneath his note is your e-mail, which your coworker forwarded to him without your knowledge or any discussion with you. Now, you feel he has tried to make you look bad, and you wonder how he presented the incident to your boss. Does your boss think you're the villain? Your first instinct is to be even angrier at your coworker, because you were attempting to take the high road, rather than potentially getting him in trouble with the boss. In return, it appears he took the opportunity to try to get you in trouble. Rather than angrily confronting him, or storming over to the boss, you try to stay calm.

The next time the coworker passes your office, you calmly ask him if he has a few minutes to talk. He consents. You calmly say, "I received an e-mail from the boss this morning. It appears that you forwarded my e-mail to the boss. Do you and I have a problem?" The coworker is silent a moment, then says, "Yes, I did forward it, well . . ." he continues, stammering a little, "I guess I just thought he should know . . . but, no we don't have a problem, at least as far as I am concerned."

You recognize from the coworker's stammering, and from his uncharacteristically tentative approach, that he perhaps was just uncomfortable and didn't know how to approach it or what to say to you. You tell him how it made you feel when he said that, and give him a few examples of what it's like to have these challenges. He seems to listen, and he asks a few good questions that seem to indicate that he gets it.

Later on, your boss's schedule finally crosses with yours, and all he says is, "I just wanted to make sure you're okay." A short time later, the coworker tells you that you have helped him to see how he was wrong, and in the next few weeks, you see that he is making clear efforts to be respectful of your feelings. He has even incorporated some of the things you've said to him into conversations he's had with others.

While being angry at feeling made fun of is a perfectly valid reason to be upset, how accurate were some of your assumptions about your coworker's motivations for sharing the e-mail? Although you may feel that your coworker should have reached out to you proactively to apologize, what was the outcome of choosing to speak to him instead? If you had simply reported the person to HR or your boss, do you think that he would have taken the time to listen to you and learn about your perspective, or would he have been more focused on his fear that he was in trouble? In the end, is your relationship with the coworker better or worse? Is his understanding of your disability—and disability in general—better or worse?

This brings us to the second principle that has helped me deal with conflict. That is, to change how you view conflicts. Your tendency, as was mine, may be to become very focused on the things people do to hurt others. Focusing on what people should do, versus what they *actually* do, can cause frustration and anger to build quickly. But what I've learned is that this type of focus isn't productive. This is true for one basic, logical reason: You can't change the past. You can only change the present, in order to impact the future. Does focusing on what a person did wrong do anything to make your current, or future, life better? No.

Worse still, this type of focus can lead you to react in ways that, in the long run, will make your life more difficult. You begin to focus on what you have the *right* to do. "She said something really mean," you think, "So I have the *right* to say something mean right back." That may or may not be true. Many people would understand if you did. But what will be the outcome? For you and for them?

Go back to the scenario with the coworker and think about what would happen if you responded as you would have preferred. You got mad, yelled at the coworker, and called him a nasty name. Would some people understand why you did that? Yes. But you still have to work with the coworker. How easy will it be to work with him after that? Or what if the coworker did have bad intent, and now reports your behavior to the boss without discussing what he did (which people rarely do)? The boss now sees *you* as a troublemaker and unprofessional employee. Do you want that? How much harder would your working situation be after that?

Then there is the reality that you really did mistake the coworker's later intentions, when he forwarded your e-mail to the boss. The coworker is now thinking, "Wow, no good deed goes unpunished. I wanted to help her by helping the boss to understand what she explained to me in that e-mail. Now she's yelling at me and calling me names. How unprofessional!" Now your relationship is damaged with the coworker, and with your boss, too.

The next time you need a favor, or have to rely on the coworker for something that affects your job, he's less likely to help you. This, in turn, makes you less effective at your job. At the same time, the boss is now scrutinizing everything you do, waiting for you to have another outburst. This process continues to build on itself until you're absolutely miserable, and may even lose your job.

My advice in such situations is to dwell not on who is right and who is wrong but on what action will have the best impact for all involved. If you respond to bad behavior with similar behavior, the long-term impact is negative for everyone, most especially you. So when dealing with such a situation, measure the success of such a confrontation not by vindication—whether you "let them have it," or whether you're proven right—but by the end outcome, for everyone involved.

As tense as the confrontation may have been, do you understand each other better? Does he stop the offensive behavior (even if he didn't apologize)? Even if you aren't going to be best friends, is the relationship repaired enough that you can work together effectively? If the answer to these questions is yes, then that's a good outcome. You are in the workplace not to be right but to work effectively. If you preserve the relationship, you are making it easier to do so.

This is not to say that you should put up with repetitive bad behavior that rises to the level of bullying. Bullying is a big problem in the workplace, and can cause you terrible pain and stress if it is prolonged. You may be concerned reading this that handling things in this way will encourage bullies to treat you worse, but my experience has been different. It all depends on how you apply it. It takes more energy to stay calm and regulate your response, but it's worth it.

How can you use these techniques to stand up to an office bully? Sometimes it can be very straightforward. You're in a meeting when a coworker says something that sounds like it's a joke at your expense. You're not entirely sure, but you think that the coworker just implied that you're pathetic. You're upset, but you are a little bit afraid of saying something in case you're wrong. You may, in fact, be wrong. You may also, just as likely, be right. You'll never know unless you ask.

If the coworker does mean you harm in what she said, she's counting on your confusion and reticence to say anything. This works in her favor. She gets away with bad behavior unquestioned, and she can later use your nonresponse as further evidence of what she said. "See," she can tell others then, "She's so pathetic she didn't even know that I was making fun of her."

You challenge this by handling it directly. You look straight at her, and say, "Excuse me, but it seemed like you just implied that I'm pathetic. Is that what you *really* meant to say?" This puts her in a difficult position. Now, she has to answer you. Someone who really cares about your feelings will react to this kind of question immediately, and with concern. She'll say something like, "Oh, no! I certainly didn't mean to make you feel that way. I'm so sorry!" She may even come back later to check in with you to confirm that she didn't mean it in that way, and try to assess if damage has been done to the relationship so that she can repair it.

A coworker who did have bad intentions will typically answer in one of a few ways. She may respond by saying, "No, of course not! How could you think that?" She'll try to say it in a way that sounds nice, but she's being a phony. She is trying to lie to protect herself from having to admit to bad behavior. In the short term, it's hard to tell the difference, but her future behavior will confirm her true intentions. Someone who means well, and realizes that she has hurt you, will show concern for having done so, and will make a concerted effort to not repeat the same mistake. She might still make a few, but she'll be quicker to recognize them. Someone who doesn't have good intentions won't change her behavior.

Another response that a coworker with bad intentions might give you is, "Now, c'mon, I was just teasing. You're being too sensitive! Get over it!" This is not the response of a person who cares about your feelings. It is a defensive response. It shows that she knows she was wrong, but tries to distract you from this by attacking the validity of your feelings, to try to make you look like you're in the wrong. When you think about it, she did answer your question, because she didn't deny what she said. Someone who cares about your feelings will try to find out why you feel as you do, not make fun of it or dismiss it.

A third type of response you might receive is the most hurtful and blatant. The person will simply say something like, "Yes, I did. What's it to you?" or "Yes, I did. Do you have a problem with that?" In this case, there's no doubt anymore. This person not only has bad intentions but is being a true bully at this point. He is publicly calling you names and showing utter disregard for your feelings about it. If he is that blatant, then this is the time to firmly tell him exactly how you feel about his behavior.

You can say something like, "I don't think that's appropriate behavior or a respectful way to treat a coworker. I wouldn't treat you that way (if you say this last part, make sure it's true)." Or you can say, "Yes, I do have a problem with that. I think it's inappropriate and disrespectful behavior. Please stop." If you can, get away from this person. If the coworker persists beyond this point, or continues to treat you disrespectfully, he has now publicly shown to others his bullying behavior. He won't be able to accuse you of misunderstanding, because you asked, and he answered it affirmatively. So if you're forced to escalate the matter to HR or the boss, then there is no doubt.

Remember, staying calm and firm in these kinds of situations does not mean that it's wrong to get upset or angry at this treatment. Anger is like a warning light on your car's dashboard. It's an emotion that indicates that something is wrong and needs to be addressed. Listen to it, and take action. But it will be easiest and most effective to plan the best course of action when you're calm, so try to use some of the techniques discussed earlier in the book to calm yourself prior to taking that action. Anger and lack of emotional control are two weapons that bullies will use against you, either to push you into doing something out of anger, which isn't in your best interest, or to use that emotion to try to make you look bad. Don't help him do it. Beat him at his own game.

If this type of thing becomes a pattern, privately take notes about exactly what, when, and where such things happened, and save examples of taunting e-mails or other corroborating evidence. Keep it in a private place, and try not to let your coworker realize that you're doing it. If he thinks you're building a case to get him into trouble, he may increase his behaviors, which is an outcome you don't want. This information will help you in any meetings with your boss and HR. If you bring the information into a meeting where you discuss these events, make sure you take copies. You want to still have originals if the person asks to see the information, loses it, or tries to cover up what's happening.

Diplomacy

For the more direct among us, diplomacy and its related skill, tact, can be difficult. However, developing your skills in this area can help you a great deal in the workplace. These two skills rely heavily upon thinking about how what you say impacts other people, and on trying to understand others in the same way you hope they will understand you. You may prefer to be blunt and direct, but others may see it as criticism, insulting them, or putting them down. In the workplace, what gets you heard is often not *what* you say but *how* you say it. To help you figure out the right approach, here are a few points to consider:

- Recognize that others have different knowledge, needs, skills, abilities, and styles than you do, and that's okay. Everyone has something to contribute, even if it's different. If you want your contributions to be valued, then value the contributions of others.

- Remember that a trait that you feel is neutral may not be perceived by others this way. For example, you say, "Joe isn't a very social guy." You think that's a neutral statement, because that's the way you are. Others may think you're insulting Joe.

- If you see an issue with a process or product, it isn't always best to say so directly. People are proud of what they do. If you try to help them by pointing out issues or errors, they may take this as your insulting their work (and them), rather than trying to help them make it better. Instead, help them to figure it out for themselves.

- Sometimes it's best to give other people the credit.

- Always try to get a sense of what a person knows, and what he doesn't, before you try to explain a concept or issue to him. This indicates to what level of detail to explain the topic, so that you don't insult him by speaking to him as if he knew less than he actually does.

These rules have helped to make a lot of my interactions with my coworkers easier. Most coworkers like to know that you respect them, and that you respect their contributions. Do your best to let them know that you do. If you get frustrated at something they don't know how to do, or knowledge they don't have, remember that there are things that you don't know, too. How would you want them to treat you when you don't know something?

Two particular applications for these rules are when you are in a meeting, where you are trying to bring up a flaw in another person's process, or when you know something that a person whose job it is to know that piece of information clearly doesn't. These are instances in which a person's pride is at stake. Embarrassing coworkers (or clients) publicly is a way to get excluded from good projects, disliked, or even fired. In these instances, I think of it as a courtesy to try to help them come to the right conclusion, so that it looks like the knowledge or decision was theirs. In some Asian cultures, this is called "saving face." In these situations, it may mean not acknowledging what you know.

For example, you're working on a project that relies on data from another system. Because you've seen the quality of data that typically comes out of this system, you know it will cause major issues in your system. You need to get the system's owner to make changes to improve the quality of her data, but you know she's prideful and protective of her systems. She doesn't like to be told that there are things wrong with her system. What do you do?

You could say, "We need to pull data from your system, but it's junk. There are empty fields and all kinds of duplicates. We need you to fix it." But if you do, her immediate reaction will be to defend herself and challenge the degree of the statements you're making. At this point, she will be more focused on defending the job she's done in maintaining the data than she will be on fixing issues, which is what you need her to do. You may have been truthful, but this approach produces the wrong outcome.

In Our Own Words

I've learned that no matter how good you are, someone will always be out to get you. The best defense is to simply be polite and likeable because then people can't turn opinion against you. To do this, you really have to let go of many of your battles. You may think that a certain policy or choice is stupid, but you can't say it because people think that you're implying that they're stupid. —Gavin Bollard

How do you get her to do what you need her to do? You help her "save face." You describe to her what you need for your system, and you ask if she can provide it. She may answer yes. You know that this is technically the truth. She can provide the data, but currently *not* in a way that will make your system work appropriately. So, you ask her some questions. "Our system requires user data that has a phone number listed for every person. Can your system provide that?" She says, "No, actually there are some gaps." You ask her some questions about how the process works, and you listen, even though you already know much of what she will say.

Then you ask a question about the process. "So, say you've received a form to set up Sue Smith, and you set her up. Next week, Joe Blow from another department sends you a form to ask you to set up Sue again, but spells her name Sue A. Smith. What happens then? Does a new record get set up under the name Sue A. Smith?" She replies, "Well, yes." Once you ask her enough questions like this, sooner or later she'll come to the realization you already have—that she needs to fix her system, but you allow her to realize that and admit to it in her own time and on her own terms, rather than embarrassing her and making her feel shamed into doing it.

Another situation in which you may need to do this is when a coworker isn't knowledgeable in something that he should be. Imagine you're on a conference call with a number of your coworkers, and with a number of users of a system your team maintains. A user asks a question, which you know the answer to. However, instead of jumping in to answer it, you leave the answer to Jane, who was recently hired to handle that aspect of the system. But a few seconds pass, and there is silence on the phone. Either Jane isn't paying attention, or she doesn't know. You don't want the user to get frustrated that he didn't get his question answered and think that your team is incompetent, so you say, "I think that those addresses are pulled from our central address database . . . Is that right, Jane?" By asking her to confirm the information, you also make it clear that Jane is the right person to ask about these things. This way, the users don't come to you later, which could be perceived as undermining Jane's authority. Now, she also knows how to answer such requests in the future, and she wasn't embarrassed in the process of learning information she probably should have already known. If you use e-mail or instant messaging software, you could also quietly send the information to Jane via this format, so that others are less likely to realize that she is stuck.

Most coworkers will appreciate getting some help along the way, and will reciprocate by helping you when you struggle. Some will take advantage, but if they do, most good bosses will pick up on that sooner rather than later. In the end, if you want a good relationship with your coworkers (and a good relationship with coworkers will consistently make your life easier), then embarrassing them in public isn't the way to do it. If you can correct them, or help them get something done—without embarrassing them—that's the best way to go.

Clarify

Being clear in your communications is important in the workplace. Lack of clarity can cause big problems, especially when you're working with others. It's important to be very aware of your audience and what they know, and take that into account when communicating. There is a quote, often attributed to Albert Einstein, which says, "Everything should be made as simple as possible, but not simpler." This applies to communication, as well.

When speaking to someone who doesn't share your specialty, try to keep your language simple. Don't use words that are only used by specialists. If you're talking about a complex concept to a mixed group of people, start by defining a concept at a high level, and then break it down into smaller concepts. Be systematic about how you communicate, and check in with the listeners frequently to ensure that they understand you correctly. Invite them to ask you questions by saying, "Please, stop if I am saying anything that doesn't make sense."

If it's clear they're struggling, start again and begin at a more basic level. Say, for example, you're describing how to build a house to people who know very little about the process. You assume that everyone knows about laying the foundation of a house, so you don't talk about the process of laying the foundation, or even what a foundation is. Meanwhile, you're describing things that will be bolted to the foundation, etc. They are confused, what is this foundation thing you keep mentioning? This is the time to break your concept down to a more basic level. This may be a simplistic example, but I hope you get the idea.

Just like when dealing with conflict, asking questions is crucial for clarity. Often, we make a lot of assumptions about what other people know about what we are thinking. We may walk up to someone and say, "Did you get my e-mail?" assuming that she will know exactly which e-mail you mean. When this happens, it's a good idea to ask clarifying questions. You can say something like: "If you mean the one about Peter's party next Friday at six, then, yes, I did." Or I might say, "I assume you're talking about the e-mail you sent about the urgent report you need? Yes, I did and I'll take care of it right away." Clarifying questions can avoid a lot of frustration and confusion.

Office Politics

In an ideal world, doing your job should only be about accomplishing the duties you've been assigned, and then that should be rewarded. Unfortunately, that isn't always the case. Sometimes, social dynamics can create specific difficulties in getting the job done. Many times, you realize office politics are at work when you notice that something in the workplace is going on that doesn't make sense.

You may try to change a process that's costing the company money, only to be told by your boss to stop. Or, you find that the machinery or process you designed that had worked previously suddenly doesn't work, and without an obvious reason. Or you may see someone—who obviously has no qualifications to do a particular job—is given a job instead of someone with fifteen years' experience and a solid track record of success.

The reasons for office politics are often not immediately apparent. Many times, you'll find out about them later. If you're lucky, a friend, your manager, or a mentor may help you to understand the invisible barrier you're encountering. It could be that the process you're trying to change is a favorite of a senior executive. It could be that your process or machinery suddenly doesn't work because one of your coworkers is insecure and afraid that the great work you did will make him look bad, so secretly he tampered with it to make you look bad instead. It could be that the incompetent person who gets hired for a specific position is the son of the CEO.

Office politics are something you will encounter in nearly every workplace. There is little you can do to prevent them, but you can watch for patterns. If you run into unexplained issues on several projects or tasks, are there any commonalities between those incidents? Was a specific associate somewhere around when the issues occurred? If so, would there be any reason why the associate would want to make you look bad? What would he have to gain if you're fired? Might he get your job?

Once you realize what is happening, you'll need to make a conscious decision as to how to handle it. Can you prove that the coworker did harm to your program? If not, can you find a way to protect your program so that the person won't have the access to do it again? These situations are often tricky because it can be very difficult to prove his sabotage, and making accusations without proof will only make it look like you're trying to deflect blame to someone else for a mistake you made. This is what these types of people count on.

Dealing effectively with office politics is often like defensive driving. Defensive driving recognizes that you will share the road with people who go too fast, tailgate, and run red lights. Defensive driving techniques teach you how to react to protect yourself so you won't have an accident. In the office, you'll run into people who are incompetent, people who don't tell the truth, and people who try to sabotage you. The best you can do is to make sure you react to such dangers appropriately, and prevent them, whenever possible.

Some general "defensive driving techniques" for office politics include the following:

- Notice who the boss likes. Who does he/she listen to most often? When you see who those people are, be careful to treat them well. One bad word from a boss's favorite can mean saying bye-bye to your job.

- Pay attention to taboo topics. Are there specific programs or topics that seem to be off-limits for discussion? Try to figure out why. It may be because this program or topic is a "sacred cow" to a senior leader. If so, you might want to think carefully about pushing for a change.

- Choose your battles. Always consider the cost of pursuing a perceived problem or inequity. If the barriers you face in trying to overcome it are greater than the rewards you might gain, it may be time to let go of it. Also, there are times when you may consciously choose to give in on a lesser point of agreement in order to gain agreement on a larger point.

- Focus on your own performance, not other people's. Sometimes it may seem that people are not being treated consistently. As unfair as it may seem to you, you may not know all the facts. Maybe there are legitimate reasons for this perceived inconsistency that you don't know about. Maybe a coworker is allowed more flexibility with her schedule than you are because she has to accommodate chemo treatments. Because such a thing is confidential, the boss won't be able to tell you this. It may well be that she has been reprimanded privately. You don't know. You're best to focus on doing your own job, and doing it well, rather than complaining about the activities of others.

Adapting to Your Challenges

Everyone in the world has gifts and everyone has challenges. Those of us on the spectrum simply have different challenges and different gifts. In order for you to be successful, you will need to find ways to overcome or adapt to the challenges your differences create in your work environment.

Sensory Issues

For many adults on the spectrum, sensory issues are a real challenge in the workplace. Many offices have fluorescent lights that can be overwhelming. Open office plans create environments where sounds can cause you difficulties. If you have problems processing auditory input, you may have trouble understanding what is being said on a conference call or in a meeting.

To address these issues, you'll need to assess the extent of your challenges and identify potential solutions. What works is a little different for everyone. Some adults on the spectrum find that lights cause them such difficulties that they need to wear sunglasses all the time. Others find that tinted glasses, or *Irlen lenses,* help them. Others are helped by being allowed to use an incandescent light on their desk, or wearing a hat with a brim. It really depends on what works for you.

When it comes to auditory issues, it's extremely helpful if you can get an office with a door. If these aren't standard, it may mean requesting one as an accommodation. This may or may not be an option, depending on the position and organization you are in. Another option is to ask your manager if you can wear headphones or earbuds as you work. This is acceptable in many environments. You can often get a sense of how acceptable it may be by looking around and seeing what other people are doing. Are a lot of them wearing earbuds?

If you are allowed to wear earbuds, you have a lot of options as to what will work for you. You could play a CD or MP3 player, or listen to an online radio service like Last.FM (*www.last.fm*), Pandora (*www.pandora.com*) or Tune In Radio (*http://tunein.com*). If you really need to focus, you can listen to environmental noises or white noise, using applications like ChatterBlocker (*http://chatter blocker.com)* or sites like Rainy Mood (*www.rainymood.com*). If you need something a little stronger, I have heard some good reviews of the b-Calm Audio Sedation Systems (*http://b-calm sound.com/b-Calm/*).

Another solution that's available in some workplaces is telecommuting. Some companies will allow you to telecommute 100 percent of the time. Others will allow you to telecommute a few days a week. Depending on your workplace, it may be as simple as asking your boss if you can telecommute. In other workplaces, there is a formal program where you may need to fit certain criteria (length in job, for example), fill out paperwork, and sign a telecommuting agreement. If you have the ability or discipline to keep yourself on track, have a good location to work at, and can control the noise in your home environment, telecommuting can be a great way to minimize the impact of sensory differences.

If you have trouble hearing on the telephone, you may be able to use services like TTY, or you may be able to request a special telephone that allows captioning of your calls. Like TV captioning, the captioning service is only as good as the people who transcribe the captions, but if you're struggling with hearing on the phone, these services can help. If a special phone isn't an option, or you only need to use the service in certain situations, you can sign up for WebCapTel service. This is a web-based service that allows you to see the captions for your phone call right on your computer screen. You don't need any special equipment, only a computer with a browser and Internet access. Here are a few of these services: Sprint CapTel (*www.sprint800.com*), AT&T WebCapTel (*https://captel.att.com*), Hamilton WebCapTel (*www .hamiltonwebcaptel.com*), and Clear Captions (*http://clearcaptions .com*). Many of these services also provide apps for the iPhone, iPod, iPad, and other mobile platforms, so you can see captions for your cellular calls as well.

If you have trouble following conversations in meetings, you might consider using a voice recorder, so that you can go back later and review what was said, once you're in a quieter environment. This may be uncomfortable for some people, so you might want to give them the courtesy of notifying them that you'll be recording the conversation (in some cases you might be legally mandated to do so). One tool I have found useful is the LiveScribe smartpen (*www.livescribe.com*). This pen captures your writing digitally, along with what was being spoken when you wrote it. So, if you're in a meeting and you're taking notes, but you miss a word someone said, you don't have to worry about it. Later, after the meeting, you can hear the whole conversation played back again.

Organization and Executive Skills

Organization is a challenge that can be addressed in many ways with technology. Using tools, such as Outlook, can be really helpful if you have problems with working memory that make it difficult for you to keep all your pending tasks in your mind at one time. You can break down tasks into categories, which helps you to "block" tasks by type. You can set aside a half-hour for phone calls, another for e-mails or paperwork, etc. This helps you to work more efficiently, and makes it easier for those of us who work better focusing on one thing at a time. Instead of breaking it down to one task, you focus on one *type* of task.

This is just one way you can use technology to help compensate for working memory and executive function issues. You'll need to see what works for you. You may find that Outlook is too simple a tool for you to effectively plan bigger tasks that have many components. If you do, using project management software, such as Microsoft Project, may help. This software will allow you to break down one project into sub-tasks, and you can build in dependencies so that if you have to reschedule one task, it will automatically reschedule the rest. This type of software is meant to support full project management, including tracking the cost of a project and staffing requirements, but I've found it can be extremely helpful even when you're dealing with a small, one-person project as well.

To figure out what's available to you, just ask your IT department what kind of time management or project management software is available. If you're in your own business, you can use whatever you want (and can afford). Take a look at reviews online and see what software gives you the features you need and want, for the price you want. Also, don't forget that there are ways that you can sync Outlook and similar programs to a mobile device. This can really help you when you're away from the office.

Other Issues

I've covered only a few of the kinds of challenges you may encounter in the workplace. For more thoughts, ideas, and information about the types of challenges you may experience on the job, see the book *Asperger's on the Job: Must-Have Advice for People* with *Asperger's or High Functioning Autism and Their Employers, Educators, and Advocates* by Rudy Simone. Developing Talents, referenced in the chapter on career planning, also covers some of these challenges.

Additionally, try to keep up on assistive technology that could help you with your specific challenges. Unfortunately, most autism-focused assistive technology articles and lists are skewed toward technology for children, because so many people associate autism with children. You may have better success searching for technology options for people with ADD/ADHD, or for people with acquired brain injury. These conditions have some significant overlap with autism in terms of things like working memory, attention, and executive functioning, and they may yield workable options. Don't limit yourself. Regardless of what the technology is sold for, if it can help, use it.

Disclosure

For many, disclosure in the workplace, at least at some level, has helped them. Just as we discussed in the chapter on interviewing, however, there can be some specific drawbacks. People can be intolerant, and they can jump to a lot of conclusions about you based on assumptions they hold about autism. The difference between disclosing once you have a job, versus when you're interviewing, is duration of the consequences. You can't take away knowledge, once it's given. If you tell a prospective boss in an interview, and he doesn't hire you, then that's the end of it. But, if you tell when you are on the job and your boss reacts poorly to the disclosure, you have to live with the consequences. If the disclosure goes well, then that's wonderful. If not, you could find yourself in a really stressful position.

Personally, I have had the most success with partial disclosure, the "I'm the kind of person who . . ." type disclosure. However, this type of disclosure does not allow for you to file for accommodations for your disability, such as some of the assistive technology we've discussed in this chapter. If you want to request accommodations on the job, you will have no choice but to disclose. Many employers will require that you submit a doctor's note proving your disability as well. This can feel like a really uncomfortable violation of privacy, but if you feel that accommodations will make the difference between success and failure in a job, by all means do whatever you need to succeed.

Getting Support

Any social environment can be a lonely one when you're different. The workplace is no exception. There will be times when you feel you need support. The wider support base you have, the better off you'll be. When you find yourself in a difficult situation, it's a good thing to have someone you can turn to who doesn't report to the same person you do, or who isn't in the same department as you are. Lack of a support system can mean vulnerability. Vulnerability can attract predators, like bullies.

To prevent this, you'll need to find some places where you can connect to others, whether it's through special interests or through trying to grow your career. In many organizations, there are extracurricular activities like sports, band, or a chorus. Find something that works for you, and something where you can get to know others and/or get to demonstrate your ability.

Is there a forum for people in your particular type of job? If not, why not start one? This will allow you to hear the experiences of others, to share best practices, and to learn from others who may have already faced the same challenges you are dealing with. In many organizations nowadays, this doesn't even have to happen in person. Many employers today use internal social media tools to keep connected to one another. If your organization has a platform like this, see if you can connect with people like you.

One particular form of support you may want to seek out is a mentor. A mentor is someone who is senior to you who can guide you and help you be successful. A good mentor will help you to learn, and may be able to help you identify and navigate through office politics. Many adults on the spectrum reported that mentors were crucial.

In Our Own Words

Having a mentor—someone you can look up to, follow the example of, and ask difficult questions of—is a must. Your mentors need to be very honest with you—even when it hurts, and they need to be the sort of people who understand your social difficulties and will give appropriate signals to help you find your way. —Gavin Bollard

How do you find mentors? First of all, check the list of resources you built through the job search process. Who helped you find out about the job? If it was someone other than your manager, he or she may be willing to be your mentor. In this case, though, be careful if your mentor and your manager are really close. For a mentor, you want someone who can be objective, who can give you an honest opinion. If your mentor is close with your manager, works for him or her, or is even in the same department, this person may feel inhibited from giving you an honest answer about things that are important.

Another way you can go about finding mentors is by working through your company's associate resource groups (ARGs), also sometimes known as employee resource groups (ERGs), or business resource groups (BRGs). These are associate groups set up around a particular demographic or interest. Different organizations vary, but there may be networks for women, ethnic minorities, those interested in environmentalism or a specific religion, those of different sexual orientations and gender identities, those of different ages, those with disabilities, or associates who are veterans.

For the groups that are based on things like gender or ethnicity, you don't necessarily need to be of that gender or ethnicity. You need only to be interested in learning and supporting the interests of people in that group. Many of these groups set up mentoring programs that will match you with an appropriate mentor. If your organization has a resource group for people with disabilities, try getting involved with it. Meet other people with disabilities in your organization. Find out from them which areas are welcoming to people who have differences, and those that aren't. They may be able to help you understand the process necessary for requesting accommodations, and give you tips about how to survive in the company's culture. Some organizations, like the U.S. Census Bureau, have associate networks specifically for employees with autism.

Another organization you might consider joining is Toastmasters (*www.toastmasters.org*). Toastmasters is all about learning things, such as presentation skills, interview skills, and other leadership skills. It is meant to be a very supportive environment, even for those who are really nervous about public speaking. Many larger organizations have an on-site chapter. I've heard from a few adults on the spectrum that their involvement in the program helped them a great deal.

Figuring Out Ways to Get Noticed

One of the best ways you can set yourself up for success is to find ways to get noticed. In an organization, the more people know about your abilities, the better off you are. It's harder for someone to argue against you, if people have seen your capabilities first hand. Find ways to show what you can do. If another associate asks you for help in an area you're good at, help her. You'll be surprised how fast people will realize that you are someone who has valuable skills.

Know what you do well, and find ways to do it that add value to your company and your department. Just because it isn't in your initial job description doesn't mean that you can't find a way to do it. And when you do it, you often find that good things happen.

POINTS TO REMEMBER

- Etiquette rules are practiced to show respect for others in any situation you are in.

- Most companies have written guidelines regarding how to dress. It's a good idea to get a copy of these guidelines and follow them to the extent that you can.

- There may be some instances where you are able to get accommodation in order to allow you to avoid wearing clothing that negatively impacts you sensory issues.

- Most employers will expect you to respect "the niceties, which can be broken down into two groups: indications of courtesy and indications that you're thinking of others.

- Learning to resolve conflicts is important to success in the workplace.

- Choose your response to stressful situations based on what will likely result in the best overall outcome for you and everyone else, not on what you have the right to do.

- When it comes to communicating, *how* you say what you say is often more important than *what* you say.

- Use tools and technologies as much as possible to adapt to the challenges you face with sensory issues, executive skills, and other typical spectrum challenges.

- When you're at work, try to build a support network. This can include contacts you make through clubs, associate resource groups, or mentors whom you seek out in the organization.

- Try to find a way to show your skills and abilities in the workplace, even if it isn't part of your typical job description. Watch successful employees in your organization for ideas.

CHAPTER 10

Meeting and Making Friends

Friendship—it's a common discussion point when it comes to autism. If you were diagnosed early, it's likely you've heard it discussed over and over by your family and teachers. Some families treat friendship as the holy grail of successful living for a person with autism. How do you feel about it? That's important to know.

There are some people on the autism spectrum who report that they have no interest in friends and that they prefer to be alone. Others feel loneliness to the point of despair. Still others desperately want friends, but the effort it takes and the emotional cost of maintaining such a relationship is so high that they resign themselves to being alone. I have been in each of these groups at different points in my life. It all depends on what your needs are in that given moment and the energy and skills that you have available.

In this chapter, we'll discuss friendship. Where are some places you could seek friends? How do you keep them, once you have them? What about the emotional cost of losing friends, once you have them? Most importantly, we'll discuss what you need to do to make sure you're in the right emotional state to have friends.

In one well-known sitcom, one of the major characters said that having more than four friends at a time was too stressful. I laughed aloud at this, because this has been my reality for most of my life. In fact, until recently, my max was three, and these friendships probably did not look "typical" to an average neurotypical person.

I had friends who were much older, or much younger, or of the opposite sex. Older friends often shared more of my intellectual interests, and were more patient. Younger friends would look up to me and wouldn't be as critical as kids my own age. I got along with boys because they were more direct than girls, I didn't have to guess at what they thought, and they valued accomplishments, such as who built the best fort, instead of how well you socialized.

Later, I found friends based on my special interests, whether it was connecting with someone who loved animals, science, theater, or learning languages as much as I did. In these relationships, conversation was structured around these topics, and typical socializing was secondary. When, in high school, my special interest in languages became really strong, it drove me to seek out new relationships—with the exchange students in the schools that I went to.

Although I found friends, I often lacked the skill and confidence to maintain friendships. I could socialize well in certain narrow sets of circumstances, but then out of nowhere, a gap would appear in my skills and suddenly, I didn't know what to do.

If I were to pinpoint the one thing that changed my experience of friendship in adulthood, it would be learning about autism. Just knowing the difference between neurotypical people and myself has helped a great deal to mitigate misunderstandings, and to help me understand why people react the way they do. Beyond that, by becoming active in the autism community, I have garnered a number of great contacts and people whom I consider friends—even those I've never met.

All in all, I think few would look at my social life as typical, but for me it works. Every now and again, I have a moment when I realize how far I've come, and how what I've learned has changed me. Not long ago, a former colleague and friend of mine e-mailed me with a question about a type of technology frequently used in our industry, and she hoped I might be able to explain it. We set a time to talk on the phone. She called me, we exchanged a few pleasantries, and then we got to talking about the question she had asked me.

An hour or so later, I found myself talking with her about her family and mine, her experiences and world travels, and what was going on in my life. When we finally hung up the phone, I had a funny feeling, and sat analyzing it for a moment. *I was happy.* I realized for the first time in years that talking on the phone in an unstructured way was not only enjoyable but relaxing. I felt supported and connected. That's when I thought, "Wow! This must be what it's like for neurotypical people. *No wonder they like it!*"

Who Needs Friends?

As discussed in the introduction, there are a number of viewpoints in the autism community when it comes to friendships. Friendship is something that neurotypical parents often push a great deal, because friendship is extremely important in the neurotypical world. What do you do if you are a person who doesn't want friendships, and prefers to be alone?

Well, this is one of the areas in which much of the prior discussion in this book about self-knowledge and boundaries comes into play. If, after expanding your self-knowledge, you find that you are not at all interested in friendships, then this is the point at which it's appropriate to set boundaries with people who do not respect that. There are some in this world who have a hard time understanding if you don't want friends. You'll need to make sure that they understand what your true preferences are.

On the other hand, even if you are content without having the type of friendships that most neurotypical people have, you may still need some of the skills necessary in order to maintain friendships in other relationships as well, whether considered "true friendships" or not. In order to maintain a strategic partnership, for example, you'll need some of the same skills required in making friendships, and maintaining them, such as reciprocity.

The good thing about being an adult is that you are able to design your life however you want. When you set about doing that, you will have to figure out how to get all of your needs fulfilled. If your need for solitude outweighs your need for help in certain areas, you'll need to figure out a way to obtain that help in such a way that doesn't require friendship or friendship skills. Are these areas in which you could hire someone to help you? What will that cost? What is your plan for earning that amount of money? If you can answer these questions, then you have an idea as to how you can live without friends.

Most of us find that living our lives completely alone, whether desired or not, isn't always feasible. Even if you hire someone to help you with things like cleaning the house, or doing your bills, there are still some basic social skills you'll need to maintain those relationships. Although such relationships are based on work for pay, few human beings are truly satisfied with only being paid. Most people look for signs of appreciation and feel better toward a boss whom they believe has a sincere interest in them as a person. You don't have to be best friends with them, or even casual in the neurotypical sense, but friendly and considerate is a good thing to be.

What's the difference between being friends and being friendly? Friendly means being courteous and kind. It means smiling and greeting a person when you see her, and asking about her day. It means saying, "please" and "thank you" when you request someone do something. Being a friend is different. Depending on the layer of friendship, it may mean having more involved conversations, maybe about your thoughts or feelings about a specific thing, or stories about your life.

A second group of adults on the spectrum is the group that truly desires to have friendships and relationships, but who may struggle with the skills to find or maintain them. This can be extremely painful. If this is your experience, you may have tried many times to have friends and failed. You may have had brief periods of time when you did have friends, only to lose those friends. At some point you might find that you have given up. You may feel the process is so emotionally draining that you just don't have the capacity for it. You may feel worn out.

In Our Own Words

I envy those with AS who don't feel a need for relationships. My own situation, that of yearning for a sense of connection with others, but almost totally unable to achieve it, strikes me as the worst of both worlds. Better not to know what you're missing, perhaps, or at least to experience the pain of its absence less sharply.—Adult on the Autism Spectrum

If this is your situation, the plus side is that you have the interest. The important thing is to find ways to gain the skills you need to make it happen. This can take some time, so it's important not to give up, or give into despair. Just like in a boxing match, you may go through periods where you are "in the ring," finding friends and socializing. You may have times when you need to take a rest from it, to "return to your corner" in order to rebuild your energy in order to try again. Try to get to know when you're in which cycle: when you've got the energy and desire to press forward, and when it's time to rest.

Be kind to yourself, and allow yourself the rest when you need it. If you try to push yourself to be "in the ring" because you feel you're supposed to, or because you think you should be able to have the same capacity that others do, you will do damage to yourself. You may find yourself having less success than if you gave yourself the time to recover your strength. For us, friendship can be work. It can be rewarding work, but it's important to recognize your limits. Don't go into the ring exhausted.

Start with Being Your Own Friend

One of the best and most productive things you can do for yourself is to be your own friend. Learn to like yourself. Self-esteem can be challenging for those of us on the spectrum, because we've heard so many times throughout our lives from so many people what we "should do" and what we "should be." It can take us awhile to undo the damage done by all that negative feedback, both implicit and explicit.

When you're thinking of friendships, and feel sad, pay attention to what's causing it. Take some time to ask yourself what thoughts are behind the feelings of sadness. Are you thinking self-abusive thoughts? Thoughts like "Nobody likes me," or "I'm unlovable," or "I'm a jerk."? If so, try to intercept these thoughts and change them. Instead of beating yourself up, try to think about your thought patterns in terms of outcome.

If your aim is for people to like you, does calling yourself a jerk or unlovable help accomplish that goal? No—typically it would directly stand in the way of what you're trying to accomplish. Instead, try to focus on the things that are likeable about you. If there are truly negative things that prompted you to say you were a jerk or unlovable, then try to break down what these reasons are, and form a plan to address them.

For example, if you tell yourself, "I'm a jerk." Break down why you're telling yourself that. Why do you say that? You might respond, "I'm a jerk because I made a fat joke in front of Moira, and her feelings were hurt." Okay, the fact that you're sad about having hurt Moira's feelings is evidence against your *being* a jerk. Perhaps in that moment you were *acting like* a jerk, which is a different thing.

Showing remorse is the opposite of jerkiness. Now you need to address the damage you did by apologizing to Moira. You might say, "Moira, I'm so sorry I told that joke. It was really thoughtless of me. I really acted like a jerk." Perhaps, you may do some thoughtful things for her, to try to make her feel better. At this point, she may or may not forgive you, or it may take her some time to do so.

You may think that the fact that you have trouble making friends means that you're unlikable. It may mean that you haven't met the right people yet. It may be that others misunderstand your body language and style of communication as signs that you're not interested in being friends with them. Sometimes the smallest changes can make a big difference. Focus on skills. Focus on what you need to know. Don't turn a lack of skills into a character flaw. It's not.

Another way to treat yourself well is to accept yourself and have confidence in yourself. The world often teaches us that what works for us—how we think or how we express ourselves—is wrong, and that we're wrong for feeling that way. If you get down on yourself, remind yourself of all the good qualities you have. Don't try to be something you're not. You will never feel good about yourself if you constantly feel that you have to be someone else.

If you continually struggle with self-esteem, you might want to consider getting some counseling to help with this. Low self-esteem is an under-recognized problem, but a big one for making friends. Not only can it make it harder to have friends, but it can also set you up to be hurt by the friends you get. Unfortunately, there are abusive people out in the world who will take advantage of a person with low self-esteem, because they see them as good victims. It's not a pretty or a just reality, but it's true. Self-esteem is not just about making you feel good, it's also about keeping yourself safe.

The Traits of a Good Friend

When you set out to make friends, take some time to strategize. Think about what you want in a friend. There are some traits that are crucial in just about any friendship, such as respect, thoughtfulness, and caring. There are others that are more specific. Do you want someone to enjoy and watch sports with? Or someone who will enjoy reading about obscure Russian literature? What traits are most important to you?

You want to avoid exploitative people. Does a friend only want to spend time with you when he needs something? Does he offer you friendship conditionally based on your doing something or giving something? If so, he is not the type of friend you want. Friendships happen because a person enjoys spending time with you, not because you can do a better PowerPoint presentation than she can or because you buy her lunch. Beware of accidentally appearing this way yourself. Try to be aware of the ratio of things people do for you versus what you do for them. Try to keep it roughly equal if you can.

Watch how your friend acts toward others. Does he act nicely to people, but then make fun of them or say nasty things when they're not around? This is also a mark of a bad friend. If he does this to others, he will do the same to you. The same applies if you witness the person lying. A person who routinely lies to others will lie to you.

A friend should be concerned about your feelings, and should respect them. You should not be afraid to ask for what you want. If the person disagrees with some of what you ask, or feels it's unfair, she will talk to you about it. Never settle for a friendship in which a friend demands rights that she is not willing to reciprocate. This is exploitation, not friendship. Someone who insists you treat her in a way that she is not willing to treat you is someone who's not likely to be a good friend. Insist on respect in all of your relationships.

Strategies for Finding Friends

Finding friends can really happen anywhere you have the opportunity to talk to people. Personally, I have had the most success in my adult life in finding friends through work, and based on what I've heard from others on the spectrum, my experience isn't unique. Many on the spectrum find their job through their special interest, and their friends the same way. Another option is to join a club or group structured around a special interest. Sites like Meetup. com (*www.meetup.com*) list schedules and events in many different areas of interest that are open to join.

Another great place for making friends is through support groups for people on the spectrum. Many adults have reported that they found it much easier to make friends with other people on the spectrum than with neurotypical friends. Many of these groups are listed on Meetup.com, or you can go to an organization such as *http://grasp.org* and find out if they have a group in your area.

Just as it can be useful in finding a job, volunteering can be a good way to find friends as well. The people you meet on a volunteer assignment will often share interests with you, simply because you both care about the same charity or issue. This can help you to form a connection quickly. This is also true of places of worship.

Social media has also become a great tool for finding friends. In fact, you might consider social media to be an accommodation in terms of friendship. Many people on the spectrum find that the biggest issue with interacting with others is the time it takes for us to do so effectively. When pressed to come up with an immediate answer to something, we may answer instinctively in a way that doesn't help the relationship. When provided with an asynchronous way to communicate (as one online friend put it), many of us find that we're much better able to respond in a way that helps the relationship.

Sometimes, interacting with someone online for a while before meeting in person can help, because interacting online allows the other person to get to know you first in a way that makes it easier for you to communicate the most important things about who you are. By the time that you meet one another, the other person may not be as likely to judge you by your differences, because he or she has already seen enough of you to dispel any preconceived stereotypes.

If you do use online resources to find friends, or other relationships, you'll need to keep in mind a few safety guidelines:

- *Never* give out your address online.

- If you travel somewhere, be very careful where you share that information. If you post that you're going on a trip to visit your grandma in another state, some people may look up your address and take the opportunity to break into your home.

- If you choose to meet someone in real life, whom you only know through the Internet, make sure that you meet in public, and do so a few times before you trust this person with your address. Some people use the anonymity of the Internet to lure unsuspecting people into dangerous situations.

- If you can, bring someone you trust—who's good at reading nonverbal signals—with you to the first few meetings. Ask the person to give you her impression of the new friend. If she tells you that "something doesn't feel right," listen to her. Better safe than sorry.

- If you can't take someone with you, it may be a good safety precaution to notify a family member or other person that you are going to be meeting someone. Tell your family member where you will be going and an approximate time you will be back.

These are just a few ideas of places where you can meet friends, but as I mentioned at the opening of this section, you can meet people just about anywhere. Be aware of the people you meet, and try to interact with people. Smile and say, "Hi!" You never know when a chance encounter might be a chance to start a friendship.

Keeping Friends

When you find the right friends, often things will develop organically. If you are both equally passionate about a common topic, you'll both enjoy the conversation. There are, however, some things you need to consider in keeping friendships.

First of all, be aware of your friend's wants and needs. Don't dominate the friendship with your own. Sometimes even if you don't think you are, you may appear to be. For example, if you tend to get excited about something and talk about it a lot, a neurotypical friend might take this to mean that you're not interested in what he has to say. To prevent this, make sure you stop periodically and acknowledge that he is there and may have something to say. You can say something like, "I'm sorry, am I going on too long? If I am, please tell me. I do tend to get passionate about these things."

Accompany this with a smile or a small laugh, and it can help put the person at ease. Some people will say "No," even if it's not true because they fear hurting your feelings. For them you might want to ask, "Are you sure?" Often this will make the person feel comfortable enough to tell you there's an issue. If he does, say, "I'm sorry. I didn't mean to dominate the conversation. What's going on with you?" Then, listen to what they have to say for a while.

Also, keep in mind how conversational patterns work. If you are having a conversation about something you are passionate about and have been going on for a while, and then get interrupted (maybe the phone rings or someone interrupts), the conversation might not return to where you left off. You may feel that you haven't finished your point or story. There are times when this is okay. If your friend has an interest in what you were saying, he will bring you back to it by asking about it. For example, he might say something like: "Stan, now what were you saying about your new puppy?"

Be careful of saying anything that could be considered as negative or insulting about the person (even if she says it herself). Especially when the friend is female, there will be times when she will say something like, "Do I look fat in this dress?" Typically, this is not a request for an honest appraisal of how she looks. She is probably feeling uncomfortable about how she looks and is looking for validation. Later on, when you become very good friends with this person, you may at some point be able to give her honest feedback with a gentle tone by saying something like, "That fit isn't very flattering to your shape. You might look better in something else," but until you know how well she will take it, it's best to stay away from responses like that.

Another common mistake to avoid is getting too close, too quickly, or emotionally smothering the person. In the early stages of a friendship, there is a period of time when you both are assessing how well you like each other, and how deep a relationship it will be. During this time, if you start calling her up all the time, or e-mailing her every day, she may be scared away from the relationship. Remember a general rule: less is more. If you went out and did something together and enjoyed it, suggest that you do something together again, once.

If she's interested, she'll say yes. She may also want to think about it. If you suggest an outing, and she doesn't get back to you right away, don't pester her for an answer. If you want to follow up once, give it at least a week. If she still says no, or she is evasive, this may mean that she is not interested in pursuing the friendship. If so, try not to take it personally, and just let it go. If there's some other reason that she is hesitant, and things change, she'll contact you. Try not to obsess on the reasons she isn't calling back.

Also, when you first make a friend, keep to more superficial topics, such as the weather, aspects of your common interest, what he did over the weekend, etc. Don't tell him about things that are extremely personal, such as your health, family problems, or sex life. In addition, avoid "hot button topics," such as religion and politics. These topics may begin to be part of your relationship later, as you build more trust. Try not to utilize a brand new friend to "lean on" for emotional support with your problems too early in the relationship. He might mistake this as your being too needy.

When you think about disclosure (in this sense, I'm thinking about any type of disclosure, not just about your diagnosis) in relationships, think about it as a triangle. A new relationship is at the tip of the triangle. What you disclose about yourself remains relatively small. As the person proves his trustworthiness as a friend, the relationship moves further along the triangle, and the scope of what you disclose will be wider. Don't disclose everything about yourself right away, before the person has shown that he can be trusted with that information.

In Our Own Words

Use autism to analyze social protocol and develop your own style and sense of humor. Autism can be used as a social benefit. —Adult on the Autism Spectrum

Another very important aspect of friendship is respecting others' boundaries. One boundary a person may set is what you are allowed to disclose to others about that person. If not explicitly stated by her, assume that anything she shares—that's even slightly personal—is something she would prefer not to be shared. If she confides in you that she's struggling with work, for example, don't tell anyone that information (especially not if you work in the same place).

These are just a few considerations about carrying on a friendship. Along with these recommendations, I'd also suggest that the etiquette books named earlier in this book are good resources to reference as well. They provide you explicit guidelines to follow in a social setting. Some people may consider the recommendations given by Emily Post and others to be too formal, but in many situations you're better off being too formal than acting disrespectfully.

Also, much of what we discussed about communication and social skills in the first section of this book will be applicable. In your social circle, watch the behavior of people around you, and see if you can recognize patterns of behavior that are social norms. This will help you to recognize what type of behavior is expected in a specific setting.

Dealing with Transitions in Your Social Circle

Those of us on the spectrum, by nature, tend to dislike change. Unfortunately, the social world is a constantly changing one. When we're young and idealistic, we often think that our friends will be our friends forever. This is rarely the case. You will have a lot of friends in your life who will come and go. You'll need to be prepared for that.

As you get older, your life experiences will change, as will theirs. Sometimes, you'll find that you won't have much in common anymore. You'll also experience this especially during certain phases of your life, such as when you transition from high school to college, when you transition from college to the working world, or when there are changes in your workplace. It's also a common occurrence when friends get married and have children.

If you've come to really rely upon a particular friend, and really care about him or her, these transitions can be hard. You may grieve over it a little more than most. That's natural. But in these situations, remember not to take these transitions personally. They're a part of life. Friends who are really good ones will keep up the relationship. Some may not. They may also connect with you later, when they're not as busy or the circumstances of their lives change.

Think about the social world as a constantly moving river. It is never static. Just try to go with the flow.

POINTS TO REMEMBER

- Some adults on the spectrum report a need for friendship; some don't.

- A person's need for friendship may change over the lifespan, or be tied to the stress involved in maintaining a relationship.

- If you don't want friends, you may still need to acquire some of the skills needed for friendship.

- Like yourself first, and treat yourself well. People will notice.

- Decide ahead of time the traits you want to seek in a friend.

- You can find new friends almost anywhere, but clubs and groups related to your interests may be a good place to start.

- Social media can help some to find friends, but be careful to take safety precautions.

- Be aware of your friends' needs.

- Don't get too close to a friend, too quickly.

- Remember that transitions in life will come, and your social circle will change. You may grieve, but don't take it personally.

CHAPTER 11

Dating and Romantic Relationships

Romantic relationships are something that many of us on the spectrum may struggle with. They can be very complex, and also very rewarding. But the process can be especially challenging for those on the spectrum. The dating world is rife with unspoken rules and expectations, and can be difficult for even the most skilled among us to navigate. Add strong feelings into the mix and it can get pretty daunting. In this chapter, we'll discuss some aspects of dating, having a relationship, and making it work.

One Partner's Experience

When looking at romantic relationships, it's important to understand what it's like for your partner, so, for this chapter, I thought I'd give you one partner's perspective—my husband's. Below he tells the story of his own experience of our relationship, some of the challenges he experienced, and what he learned along the way.

I hadn't even heard of Asperger's when I first met my wife. I knew she was quiet and shy. Many others thought she was stuck up because she was pretty, yet seemed distant—difficult to connect with. I remember in the early days we exchanged short pleasantries. After a while we started to have longer conversations, and it became clear that other people's opinions were bad assumptions based on stereotypes. I came to know that she was different.

She could be awkward around people. She was hyperfocused on certain subjects. Sometimes, a conversation was interrupted in the middle, we wouldn't reconnect for days or hours, yet she seemed to be able to pick up in the exact place we had left off. I remember being impressed with how intelligent she was. There were times she could seem as if she was wise beyond her years, yet other times she was lacking knowledge that most people would know.

I was older and worldlier in many areas and really thought that I would teach her about life and the world. The reality seventeen years later is that, in all of her knowledge and innocence, she has taught me about the world. We have certainly had our ups and downs, probably more than most couples, due to both our differences and our similarities.

Our relationship really became easier (I think for both of us) once we had a name to put to our differences—the differences between the autistic world and the neurotypical world—not so much as a label (which I know she seemingly rebels against—but not necessarily) but as an explanation for what we needed to understand.

We communicate differently. I am a sarcastic Northerner and she didn't "get" most of either my sarcasm or my jokes. So we learned how to communicate more literally. There were times when we were embroiled in heated discussions that escalated into arguments. Then we learned how to better listen and hear one another and then to ask the right questions to allow us to interpret what was being said. Ironically, it turned out many times that we were both on the same side of the argument, but the poor listening and interpreting caused the divide.

My frustrations as a type A personality would challenge my patience as she struggled to get the words out, and as the stress level rose, it would cause her to stutter and freeze up. Compounding the situation were our differing views based on my perception that she viewed everything in black and white absolutes, where I believed I saw everything in shades of gray.

There were so many misunderstandings and frustrations, like learning each others' social cues and what body language meant. My lack of patience didn't help this. There were times when I uttered terrible hurtful comments and I learned later how deeply I had hurt her. I made wrong assumptions of her motives many times because of my neurotypical paradigm. It's amazing we made it through.

At the end of it all, the label (Asperger's) gave me the parameters to understand it all. And once I understood it, I could deal with it better. My frustration gave way to understanding and compassion. I started to mellow. I remember one of our first Christmases together—she knew that I loved John Lennon and proceeded to buy me seemingly every CD he ever recorded. Yes, it was unusual, yet generous and kind.

I have watched her progress and learn and evolve to become a successful, self-sufficient, vital contributor to humanity. The autistic—or even the entire disability—community doesn't yet know what a passionate advocate it has in her. I have seen her in her darkest times. I have held, tried to comfort, and helped her through when things seemed so overwhelming. The mistaken notion that those on the spectrum do not feel or experience empathy—what a lie. I don't know anyone who feels more (good and bad) for others than she does.

The irony of this journey is that I have learned as much, or maybe more, than she has. Learning how to deal with differences has helped me to become a better listener and really learn how to be patient. She is unequivocally the best person I know (and I have a pretty extensive network) and because of this, she has made me a better person.

My fondest hope is that the readers of this book keep striving to be productive, vital people—do not give up. Help others to have the understanding they need. In their darkest days—both those on the autism spectrum and their families, caretakers, and friends— need to take the time to appreciate and understand each other.

Why Date?

First of all, let's talk about why you would want to date, or have a relationship. There are a lot of reasons, but what are yours? This is an important consideration. Even among neurotypical people, many people often feel pressure to date or have sex earlier than they really feel ready to do so, simply because they think it's the "normal" thing to do. As early as junior high, kids begin to talk about it.

In Our Own Words

Relationships don't work without work. You get out what you put in. The grass *always* appears greener on the other side but it rarely is. —Gavin Bollard

Soon, it feels as if you hear about it from everyone. You think that "everyone is doing it." Often times, though, they're not. A lot of kids may say they are, just because they don't want to be "uncool."

But even if they are having sex, that doesn't necessarily mean that you need to. They aren't you. You should decide to pursue a romantic relationship based on your own assessment of your needs and abilities, when *you* assess that you are ready.

When I first got into a relationship, it was with someone with whom I had a solid friendship first. A person who was kind, supportive, and helped me out with a lot of things. Even so, things were difficult. By nature, romantic relationships often involve really strong feelings, and those feelings can make it very difficult to deal with the ups and downs of a relationship. During those early years, the stress of the relationship actually caused a regression in some of my skills, resulting in the return of negative coping behaviors, such as self-injury.

Relationships can be great, but don't underestimate the kind of work that's involved. Make sure that you assess the reasons you want a relationship. If you want a relationship just to avoid being lonely, there may be other ways to go about it, such as pursuing a more varied social life in terms of friendships. If you want a relationship just for sex, that's probably not the best reason, either.

Whenever sex comes into any kind of relationship, strong emotions can as well. If you're not equipped to deal with those, it's not a good idea to take on that aspect of life. The ideal reason you want a relationship is that you want a truly deep connection with another human being, both emotionally and physically, and you're willing to work to make that happen.

Finding the Right Girl or Guy

Before you start looking for potential partners, try to spend some time thinking about what you might want in a partner. Ideally, start with the list of traits you'd want in a friend. You will, however, need to add some traits to that list. Think not only about now but also about the future. What do you want your future relationship to look like? Will you want to get married or have kids? If so, you'll want to think about that. It can be painful if you get serious with a partner, find out you really love him or her, and then find out that he or she doesn't want to get married or have kids.

In Our Own Words

I think it is important to find someone who accepts one for who one is, complete with quirks, stims, and social ineptitude. Sex doesn't last forever, but, I believe, love can. —Rory Patton, Adult on the Autism Spectrum

Don't make the mistake of thinking they'll change or come around to it, or that you can talk them into it. You don't want a reluctant spouse, and you don't want a spouse or partner who is a reluctant parent. He may do it because he loves you and wants to make you happy, but he may feel trapped into doing it. A person who feels trapped often acts out in hurtful ways, or finds that he is just so unhappy in such a situation that he eventually leaves you. While these are not topics to bring up on a first date, or even a fifth, they are topics to discuss before you get too involved with someone. The more feelings you have for the person when you break up, the more painful it will be.

Just as with friendship, finding potential romantic partners can happen just about anywhere. You can meet them at the gym, at a shared club, volunteer activity, or any other activity where you might find a friend. You might also try online dating services like eHarmony (*www.eHarmony.com*), Match.com (*www.match.com*), or Chemistry.com (*www.chemistry.com*). If you do, be sure that you always tell the truth on such sites, and also follow the same safety rules you would when using other social media. Don't give away any information that could help a criminal find your house, or steal your identity (such as your social security number, driver's license number, or full birthdate).

You can also choose to pursue a relationship with a current friend. This has many benefits, the first of which is that the person has already proved his trustworthiness as a friend, and you already know how you get along. The downside is that if you progress to a steady, romantic relationship with him, and develop deep feelings for him, it may be difficult to go back to a simple friendship afterward. So, choosing to pursue a relationship with an existing friend may be great, but it is possible that it could backfire if it doesn't work out.

Typically, you begin a relationship with dating. Dating involves going out for activities, such as dinner, a movie, or any activity you mutually enjoy. The purpose of dates is to get a sense of who the person is, and your compatibility as a couple. When you date, you'll talk and enjoy time together, and you may progress to kissing or holding hands, or to activities that some call heavy petting. Depending on your beliefs, you may choose to have sex. However, for many people, progressing to the point of physical intimacy often implies a sense of seriousness to the relationship.

When you're casually dating, you might continue to date other people, but many potential partners would have their feelings deeply hurt if they found out you were having sex with them and with another person during the same period of time. Also, many partners would be hurt if you begin a relationship that progressed to sex with someone else right after having broken up with the former partner. There is an assumption that if you really cared about the person, you'd be hurt by the breakup, and you would allow a period of time to grieve over the relationship. If you move right on to another relationship, it will appear that the relationship didn't mean very much to you.

This new relationship might also become something called a "rebound relationship." A rebound relationship is when you get quickly involved with someone else after a breakup with someone you really cared about, before you really have had a chance to get over the pain of the breakup. Beginning the new relationship makes you feel better in the short term, but because you haven't dealt with the pain of the breakup, you and the new partner will face additional problems. It may be, also, that you choose this partner hastily without considering his or her compatibility with you. These kinds of relationships interfere with your emotional healing from the previous breakup, and have the potential to cause some serious pain on the part of the new partner as well.

About Sex

Dr. Helen Fisher is a biological anthropologist and researcher in the area of human relationships. In her book *Why We Love: The Nature and Chemistry of Romantic Love*, she discussed three different types of love you can feel toward another human being in a romantic relationship. There is the sex drive, long-term attachment, and romantic love. Each of these states produces in your brain a different chemical reaction, and all of them can work at once, ideally with all of your energies directed toward one person, but this is not always the case.

Her research has shown that passionate, romantic love is a chemical reaction, and that chemical reaction is not unlike addiction to cocaine. When under the influence of strong romantic feelings, you cannot stop thinking about your partner, and have a drive to be with that person. You also feel acute pain if that person should break up with you. You long for your former partner as if detoxing from a drug, and will become acutely depressed. The research also found that a good orgasm during sex can release strong brain chemicals that can kick off these emotions, even if you had no idea or intention of falling in love. Because of this, she says, there really is no such thing as casual sex.

This is important to know if you decide to participate in a hook up. You may agree with someone to just have a hook up, and then find that your partner doesn't want to let you go. As those of us on the spectrum tend to be literal and believe what we are told, you may feel as if the person lied to you when he said that it would be casual. The reality may be that he thought that he could avoid falling in love, but his own biology surprised him, and suddenly he has strong feelings. It may also happen to you in reverse: that you agree to "just sex" with someone, and then develop deep feelings and find yourself in deep pain when he doesn't reciprocate.

When you make decisions on when to progress in your relationship to a sexual relationship, know that "just sex" isn't always "just sex," and that any sexual situation has the potential to become emotional. Sometimes it won't, but be prepared if it does. And, if it does and it's unwanted, be kind to the other person. Don't accuse a partner of violating your agreement and tricking you. Recognize that your partner is in pain and try to treat him or her with consideration for that pain.

Learning about the Mechanics of Sex

Some books I have read for people on the spectrum have recommended things like reading romance books or watching porn in order to learn about sex. I can't really recommend that. My early sources of learning about sex were romance novels. In the long run, I feel that hurt me. Why? Because romance novels are based on fantasy, as are porn videos. They don't reflect how sex or relationships actually happen in the real world and thus result in expectations that really don't work, or are actually damaging to yourself or your relationships.

For good resources on sex, visit the relationships section of the bookstore. There are many books on how to have good sex in a relationship, written by counselors and sex educators. Many of them also have sections on birth control, and how to use it. This is a very important topic, so make sure you educate yourself in this area. Not only is it about avoiding pregnancy, it's also about keeping yourself safe from STDs, some of which, such as AIDS, can have serious, long-term repercussions.

Safety on a Date

When you think about love or even sex, safety might not be a topic you associate with it, unless you're thinking about it in terms of the phrase "safe sex." However, physical safety is a definite concern in the dating world, especially for women. When you are dating, and you really like someone, you want to think the best of him or her. But, until you've built an appropriate level of trust, it's best to be careful. According to some estimates, 70 percent of rapes are perpetrated by someone the victim knows. This could include someone you're on a date with.

In the early stages of a dating relationship, especially if you don't know the person very well, it's good to follow some safety rules. First of all, until you really trust the person, don't go to his house, and don't invite him to yours. Don't go anywhere where you'll be completely alone. Go out to a public place, with plenty of people around. Take your own transportation so that you can leave whenever you want and you're not reliant on your date to drive. Be careful about drinking too much alcohol, which may affect your judgment, and try to be careful to avoid any situation where someone might sneak a mind-altering substance into your drink. Don't take any medications from people you don't know well.

Be alert to any signs of a violent temperament or abusive behavior in your date. If he inflicts violence on you, or even threatens it, that's a bad sign. Being obsessive about you, keeping track of your activities, and following you around is called stalking. This is something you should not tolerate. If he's cruel, excessively jealous or mean to you, or belittles you in any way, that's a sign that he may be an abusive partner. In these kinds of cases, you're better off cutting off the relationship, no matter how much you like the person. Remember, you're worth what any other person is worth. That means you deserve respect. Anyone who treats you with disrespect is not a person to keep around.

You should never treat a partner this way, either. If you do, he will be perfectly within his rights to break up with you.

Progressing in a Relationship

At some point, you will want to progress in your relationship. As discussed above, many people will consider that the relationship has become serious when you have sex, but in other situations (such as a hook up) it may not be. But there will come a time when you want to discuss whether to move on to a more serious relationship than just dating, and whether you want to be exclusive. If you really like someone, waiting for that person to decide whether to be serious with you can be really nerve-racking. However, don't rush the process. Dating is meant to give you the opportunity to get to know the person, and let him get to know you, too. If you rush it, you may wind up with a partner who isn't really right for you.

When you're in the early stages of a relationship, relax and just try to enjoy the time together. If you try to press the person for an answer, he or she may just break it off, but if you allow a potential partner time to truly learn about you and get to know you, you will have a much better result. Just as we talked about when we talked about friendship, go with the flow. Don't worry too much about every little nuance. Just be yourself. Remember, if you move onto a more serious, even permanent relationship with this person, you want that person to know you as you really are.

In Our Own Words

When I have managed to muster the courage to ask a woman out, and been lucky enough to have her accept, I always find myself struggling to decipher, and often wildly overanalyzing, every nuance of speech, motion, expression. And because I hate the inevitably ambiguous early stage of a courtship, where the party's interest is unclear, I am prone to force the question very early. And forcing a question is a good way to get a negative answer, I have found. —Adult on the Autism Spectrum

Microanalyzing every aspect of the relationship, and worrying about how it will work, is not sustainable in the long term. Neither is trying to cover up autistic traits, or being someone you're not. Choose someone you can be yourself with, and the let the relationship grow organically. If a person thinks that she is the right person for you, then she will tell you.

Making a Relationship Work

How do you make a relationship work? Well, a great deal of this is about how you communicate with and treat your partner, especially when it comes to conflict. Over several years, a researcher named Dr. John Gottman studied the differences in how couples interacted with each other. What he found, after reviewing thousands of hours of couples talking to each other, was that there were specific patterns in how couples related to each other that almost always resulted in a breakup. His study focused on married couples, but I believe it applies to just about any serious relationship. The four patterns he identified, which he calls the "Four Horsemen of the Apocalypse," are outlined here:

- **Defensiveness:** What does it mean to be defensive? It means that in an argument or conflict, you react by defending yourself rather than listening to what your partner is saying. Whenever your partner is communicating with you, your partner is communicating with you for a reason. It's your job to find out what that is. Defensiveness is counterproductive, because it stands in the way of your finding out what, exactly, is wrong and what you can do to fix it.

- **Criticism:** We've already discussed criticism in several areas of this book. What self-criticism looks like, for example, is when you say, "I'm a jerk," or "I always mess things up!" It's when you're identifying something as a character flaw, rather than as a behavior. When directed at a partner, it's about attacking them, rather than doing what an argument is supposed to do, which is to solve a problem in the relationship.

- **Contempt:** Contempt is the ultimate form of attacking your partner, aside from physical violence. When you show contempt, you call your partner names, mock, use sarcasm, or make fun of him or her. When you are showing contempt to your partner, you are showing a deep lack of respect.

- **Stonewalling:** When a partner stonewalls, it means that he stop talking or communicating at all. This disrupts the purpose of an argument, because it stops the flow of information from one partner to another. It's a less hostile way to show disrespect to your partner than contempt, but it still really stands in the way of true communication. I don't have any data on this, but I suspect that stonewalling might appear more common amongst those on the spectrum for a number of reasons. First, because a common reason behind stonewalling is being emotionally overwhelmed. Given we are already prone to being easily overwhelmed, we might be tempted to use this technique more often. Second, because another common reason for stonewalling is not knowing what your emotions are, it may be more common among those of us who have alexithymia. Third, because we may appear to be stonewalling (from a nonverbal standpoint) due to lack of typical body language, even if we are not.

What did successful couples do? First of all, according to Dr. Gottman, they were gentle with one another. If your partner does something that hurts you, try to give him or her the benefit of the doubt. When you raise an issue, raise it softly. Instead of starting a complaint by saying, "You left the fabric softener out on the counter again! I always have to ask you to put it away! You're such a slob!" Say (in a kind tone), "Honey, did you realize you left the fabric softener out? Would you mind putting it away?" By bringing up the issues as shown in the second example, you acknowledge that there's a possibility that he or she didn't mean to leave it out, and you treat your partner with respect.

Another best practice in relationships identified by Dr. Gottman's research was to take responsibility for your own failures, no matter how small. In an argument, you can get so focused on what the other person has done wrong that you forget to recognize when you're doing something that's hurtful as well. When you're talking to your partner, try to focus on doing what is best for the relationship and for the outcome of the argument in general. Remember, when it comes to relationships, it's not productive to try to be right. Blame isn't helpful. Solving the problem you both face (and the barrier to closeness it has created) is the most important thing.

In the end, what Dr. Gottman found is that the best predictor of a long-term relationship is the quality of the friendship, connection, and shared meaning you can create. This is an extremely hopeful thing for those of us on the spectrum, because it says that if we can learn to master the skills of friendship, and we find a partner who's equally passionate about what we care about (such as someone who shares our special interest), the potential for a successful, long-term relationship is high.

This is something that my relationship has shown. My best friend and I have been together for more than fifteen years and have been married for almost seven. It hasn't been easy, especially when we're communicating across neurological and cultural differences, but I can honestly tell you that when something good happens, he's still the first one I want to share it with. He makes me laugh like no one else ever has. A relationship can be work, yes, but done right, it's definitely worth it.

POINTS TO REMEMBER

- Assess why you want to have a relationship. Don't feel pressured to pursue a relationship just because "everyone else does."

- Relationships require all of the skills that friendships do, and more. If you haven't mastered the skills of friendships, relationships may be difficult. Even the best relationships require work.

- When considering the traits you want in a romantic partner, start with the traits you want in a friend. Be sure to think about the future as well.

- Online dating is an option for finding the right partner; however, you need to take proper procedures to protect yourself online.

- The purpose of dating is to allow the two of you to get to know each other and asses if you are a good couple.

- Anytime sex comes into a relationship, there is the potential that strong emotions will develop on either side.

- Books by counselors and sexual educators are better sources for learning about the mechanics of sex than are romance novels or movies.

- Observe basic safety rules when you are on dates.

- How you manage conflict is crucial for the success of a relationship.

- Successful relationships are based on the quality of connection and friendship among the partners.

Glossary of Idioms and Expressions

I wanted to include this section in the book because expressions and idioms are frequently used in many contexts, especially the workplace. Unfortunately, for many on the spectrum, they can be very confusing if taken literally. Listing every possible idiom or expression you could encounter in daily life would take an entire book, so I have gathered only a few examples, mostly from the chapters of this book. If you hear other idioms that you are not familiar with, you can always look them up in a dictionary or on one of the many reference websites that list idioms and their meanings:

- The Free Dictionary—*http://idioms.thefreedictionary.com*

- UsingEnglish.com—*www.usingenglish.com/reference/idioms/ cat/*

Besides just looking up the meaning of an idiom in a dictionary or on a reference site, there are a couple of techniques that have often helped me to remember or make sense of the meaning of an idiom. One is to look up the etymology of the phrase—the phrase's history and how it came into the English language. This will often help a seemingly nonsensical phrase to make more sense.

"After the fact"—if something happens "after the fact," it happens after an event that's being discussed.

"All in all"—considering everything. You may have had a difficult experience with something, but thinking back, find that, "all in all" (considering all aspects of the experience), you think that the experience was a good one to have had, despite its negative aspects.

"A number of"—when someone says there are "a number of" any particular type of thing, it means that there are many of them.

"Backfire"—if something "backfires," it means it has unexpected negative consequences.

"Beating yourself up"—to criticize yourself, or call yourself names.

"Blowing up"—this idiom has many meanings. You can "blow up" a balloon or "blow up" a bus. Blowing up a balloon means to fill it with air. To blow up a bus means to cause it to explode. In an emotional context, if you say that he "blew up," it means that he had an emotional outburst, usually an angry one.

"Bottom line"—a financial term referring to the line on a financial statement that shows the profit or loss of an enterprise. Often used as a metaphor for "the ultimate result" or the most important thing to consider in a situation.

"Dirty work"—to do the "dirty work" is to do the unpleasant tasks related to any type of project, or to life in general. It's often used in a context when someone is asking or requiring someone to do unpleasant tasks that are technically the responsibility of someone else, as in, "I don't want to do your 'dirty work.'"

"Get on in the world"—to navigate or manage your daily life.

"Give leeway"—to "give someone leeway" has multiple meanings. One meaning is to be a little more forgiving in a situation. It also can mean to grant a person some freedom to use her own judgment in a situation.

"Holy grail"—means the most important goal of a particular situation that people will take extreme actions to accomplish.

"I dodged a bullet"—to "dodge a bullet" is to very narrowly avoid a serious consequence. If you said something bad about your boss, and just a second later he appears, you "dodged a bullet" because he didn't hear the bad thing you said about him, and therefore won't fire you.

"Keep you on track"—to "keep on track" means to keep to a schedule or a plan, often in order to complete a particular task or project. Think about it this way, if a train is "on track," it means that it can continue toward its destination. If it's "off track," it means that it has derailed and is no longer on its way to the destination.

"Knock 'em dead"—this has nothing to do with actual violence. When you "knock someone dead," it means you impressed him a great deal.

"No good deed goes unpunished"—this is a saying people use when they feel as if they tried to do something nice for someone else, and instead of receiving gratitude, something bad happens.

"Point that out"—to "point something out" is to identify something and emphasize it. It can refer to ideas or things. If you're looking at a group of Christmas ornaments that are green, and you notice that one is red, you might point it out to a friend who likes red. If you're talking to someone about a topic you're interested in, you might point out an aspect of the topic that she hasn't heard of.

"Was my undoing"—to say that something "was your undoing" means that the thing, whatever it is, resulted in your ultimate failure or ruin.

"Sacred cow"—a term used in business to refer to a concept or project that is the favorite of a senior leader, which isn't allowed to be changed or eliminated, even if it's flawed or destructive. Origins of the term may reference the Hindu custom of treating cows as sacred (and therefore not allowing them to be killed).

"Say"—when someone says, for example, "Say you like chocolate," the person is not literally instructing you to verbalize the words "you like chocolate." In this context, "say" is synonymous with "imagine."

"Take the high road"—to "take the high road" means to do what is right when you had the option to do something that was wrong but understandable. For example, if someone yells at you, and you respond in a respectful tone, that's taking the high road. It would be understandable if you yelled back, but instead, you took the better choice.

"Torn/torn between"—to be "torn" is to be conflicted. It is used when you aren't sure which action to take of two particular options and often implies that the choice is very painful.

"To stew"—to "stew" about something is to get really angry but not express it. "Stewing" about something often results in "blowing up."

"Tune out"—to "tune something out" is to ignore, unconsciously or consciously, a particular sensory input. This can include "tuning out" to speech, not for sensory reasons, but because you don't want to hear what the person is saying. The expression comes from the use of old radios and TVs, when getting a signal required that you "tune into" the signal by turning a knob. The modern equivalent is changing the channel.

"Ups and downs"—the good and bad things that happen to one from time to time throughout one's life.

"Upside/downside"—the "upside" of a situation is the good aspect of a situation, or benefits of the situation. The "downside" is the opposite.

"Zero in"—to "zero in" on something means to quickly notice and narrowly focus on a particular thing, often a detail others might not see. If you're especially good at spelling, you might "zero in" on a spelling mistake on a big poster.

"Zero to sixty"—a reference to the measure of a car's acceleration speed that is based on the length of time it takes to go from zero to sixty miles an hour. Sometimes used as a metaphor for a quick rush of emotions that comes on suddenly.

Index

Index